SPARTACUS

ANCIENTS IN ACTION

SPARTACUS

Theresa Urbainczyk

BRISTOL CLASSICAL PRESS

First published in 2004 by
Bristol Classical Press
an imprint of
Gerald Duckworth & Co. Ltd.
90-93 Cowcross Street, London EC1M 6BF
Tel: 020 7490 7300
Fax: 020 7490 0080
inquiries@duckworth-publishers.co.uk
www.ducknet.co.uk

A catalogue record for this book is available
from the British Library

ISBN 1 85399 668 8

Typeset by e-type, Liverpool
Printed and bound in Great Britain by
CPI Bath

Contents

To the memory of
Alec Cowley

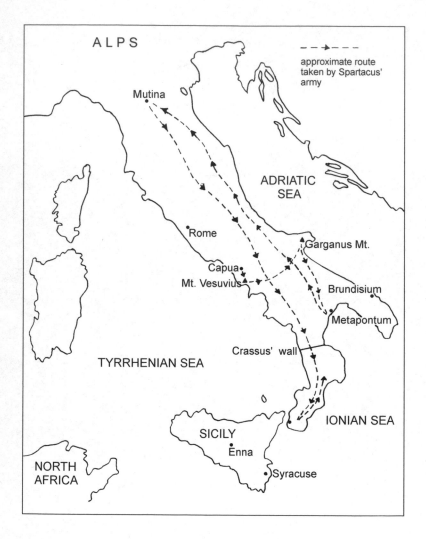

ALPS

Mutina

ADRIATIC SEA

approximate route taken by Spartacus' army

Rome

Garganus Mt.

Capua
Mt. Vesuvius

Brundisium

Metapontum

Crassus' wall

TYRRHENIAN SEA

IONIAN SEA

SICILY

Enna

NORTH AFRICA

Syracuse

Introduction

Spartacus means the fire and spirit, the heart and soul, the will and deed of the revolution of the proletariat.

Words by Karl Liebknecht, inscribed on a pillar commemorating the *Spartakusbund*, on Chausseestrasse, Berlin[1]

More than two thousand years ago, Rome was an enormous teeming metropolis. This single city had spread out its tentacles, gradually controlling the whole Italian peninsula, then the lands bordering the Mediterranean, demolishing other empires which tried to stop this progress. In a single year, 146 BC, powerful enemies were utterly crushed when Roman forces destroyed the cities of Carthage and Corinth. The Romans were the masters of the universe. Nothing could stop their mighty army; kings, empires, the natural world, all came under their dominion. When it seemed that nothing could stop this increasing imperialism, fewer than a hundred slaves proved that Rome was not invincible. The subsequent military defeats were not just unexpected and damaging for the Romans, they were deeply humiliating. Spartacus was the name of one of these slaves, and the fame of his rebellion has proved as long-lasting as the renown of the Roman Empire.

Before this story starts, however, one of the ancient sources tells us that when Spartacus was first brought to Rome to be sold as a slave, while he slept one night, a snake was seen coiled up round his face by those around him. (Today most people envisaging this face will think of that of Kirk Douglas, with its distinctive dimpled chin, although, disappointingly, this episode was not in the film.) Spartacus' wife was there as she had been captured with him. She was a seer and she interpreted the appearance of the snake as the sign of a great power that would bring Spartacus good fortune.

The word that means good fortune in Greek is 'eutyches', but it is not clear in all the manuscripts of our ancient sources, and some scholars have suggested that the word should read 'atyches' which means bad fortune. This one textual problem encapsulates attitudes to Spartacus. For some he was a hero, a man blessed by fortune who achieved great things and stands out as a beacon for all the oppressed. For others he was a tragic figure who had the misfortune not only to have failed, but never even to have had a chance of winning.

Many people today when they hear the name Spartacus think of Kirk Douglas. The influence of Kubrick's film has been enormous, but Spartacus was famous before 1960. The film was based on a successful novel, *Spartacus*, by the American writer Howard Fast, who in the mid-twentieth century was quite a celebrity, yet fell foul of the McCarthyite authorities and was jailed for his left-wing views. In prison Fast had been curious to learn about the ancient rebel because of the name of the German revolutionary group set up in 1916 by Karl Liebknecht, Rosa Luxemburg, Clara Zetkin and Franz Mehring, the *Spartakusbund* which was the precursor of the German Communist Party.

By this time, the name Spartacus was synonymous with justified rebellion. The *Spartakusbund* was established to organise opposition to the First World War, when, to the horror of some of its members, the German Social Democratic Party backed the government and the war. Liebknecht and Luxemburg were assassinated in January 1919 when their uprising failed, but they were taken up as heroes in Communist East Germany. Even after the fall of the Wall, thousands of people still bring flowers and create a carpet of red carnations at their memorial every January in Berlin.

Spartacus' fame did not start in the twentieth century. As early as 1760 a play by Bernard Saurin about Spartacus had been performed in Paris. Voltaire, one of the major figures of the Enlightenment, the age of reason, wrote in a letter in 1769 that Spartacus' war was 'a just war, indeed the only just war in history'.[2] Voltaire, although a savage critic of many aspects of life at that time, was hardly a revolutionary. Indeed he greatly admired English institutions and thought that France had much to learn from the liberties English subjects enjoyed.

By the time of the French Revolution Spartacus was acclaimed as a hero and fighter against slavery. The revolutionary ideas shaking France also affected her colonies, and in 1791 slaves revolted on the Caribbean island of Saint Domingue. Over the following ten years the slave army fought and defeated invading British, Spanish and French armies, and in 1804 the island, now called Haiti, was declared an independent republic. Slaves and slave-owners everywhere understood the ramifications of these events, and the list of slave revolts that followed elsewhere in the world is staggering. Hardly unconnected with all this unrest is the fact that between 1807 and 1820 the slave trade was abolished by Denmark, Britain, America, Spain and Portugal. In 1796 Toussaint L'Ouverture, the leader of this almost incredible slave revolt, was dubbed 'the black Spartacus' by an admirer.

The effects of the French Revolution were far-reaching. In nineteenth-century Italy they gave rise to the Risorgimento, a movement for unification which eventually resulted in the formation of the kingdom of Italy in 1861. One of the most famous characters and heroes of this period of Italian history is the general Giuseppe Garibaldi.

Although the equation of Garibaldi with Spartacus is not as obvious as in the case of Toussaint L'Ouverture, Garibaldi at least had geography on his side, fighting in the same arena, as it were. In 1848 he led sixty members of his Italian Legion back into Italy after his exile, rather reminiscent of the small number of followers Spartacus had at the start of his war. In 1849, after proposing that Rome be an independent republic, Garibaldi and his army fought off the French forces from Rome for a while, later retreating through central Italy avoiding the French and Austrian armies. The retreat can hardly be hailed as a victory, but it was seen as a sign of his great leadership.

Garibaldi was acclaimed as a general but he also understood how to win public support to great effect. In 1874 Raffaello

Giovagnoli, who had fought with Garibaldi, wrote his novel *Spartaco*. The comparison between ancient and contemporary is made explicit in the pages of this narrative. Garibaldi himself wrote an introduction to the novel. In the twentieth century the film industry has been important in purveying history to the masses. In Italy looking back to the ancient world was for obvious reasons important for this relatively young country, and films with the title *Spartaco* were released in 1909, 1913 and 1952.

Marx famously described Spartacus as 'one of the best characters in the whole of ancient history' adding 'A great general (unlike Garibaldi)'. In this judgement on the ancient slave-leader, Marx was followed by Lenin and Stalin, and the importance of Spartacus in former Communist countries is immeasurable. Even today in the area of Berlin called Friedrichshain-Kreuzberg there is a primary school named after Spartacus,[3] while the leading football team in Moscow owes its name to the slave-leader.

Thus, for related reasons, Spartacus was lionised in France, Germany, the USA and Italy and later the Communist countries. His name lives on. A quick search for the word 'Spartacus' on the internet throws up the 'System for Planning and Research in Towns And Cities for Urban Sustainability'; 'Spartacus Educational' giving help with the National Curriculum; 'Spartacus Leathers' offering all that is new in nipple clamps, Spartacus Software; Spartacus Rubgy Club, Athletics Club and even, oddly, Sailing Club; 'Spartacus Security', an international security consultancy offering counter-terrorism training; Greek (why Greek?) restaurants in the states of North Carolina and New York; a type of under-pants for men which has the advertising line 'In the race for style, you'll emerge as a true hero wearing Spartacus' and 'Camping Spartacus' near Pompeii. There are war-games based on his revolt, there are saunas and fitness centres named after him, there is the *Spartacus International Gay Guide*,[4] musicians write songs inspired by him, novelists write novels about him and there is a ballet, *Spartacus*, with immediately recognisable music for many people. And yet the facts surviving from the ancient world are rather abbreviated. He was a slave who rebelled, but who ultimately did not win. Some scholars have professed to find his cult status puzzling. Why celebrate someone who lost? He was not the only leader of a slave revolt in history.

Not a negligible reason is that he was a gladiator, a word synonymous with sex, violence and death since Roman times. Ridley Scott drew on the romantic popularity of the Spartacus-figure in his film, but he also used the glamour of the word 'gladiator'. The Latin word *gladius* means 'sword' and 'penis', and we are told that women found the games sexually exciting. There were virtually naked men sweating, fighting, bleeding and dying in front of them, and one might assume that men also had what today we might call a perverted pleasure in watching such action.

The gladiatorial games have come to symbolise Rome's asser-tion of power over other nations and human beings as well as over nature. Criminals were executed, gladiators, who might be criminals condemned to be gladiators, fought to the death in the arena, and hundreds of exotic wild beasts were also slain for the amusement of the populace. Gladiators might attract sexual attention but their status was extremely low, indeed comparable to that of prostitutes.

Although a member of this subclass, Spartacus is as famous as Julius Caesar. Far less survives from the ancient world about him than about Caesar, yet his name is still known two thousand years after he died. What was written about him was, for the most part, extremely negative. Yet he survived this character assassination to become and remain a popular hero for twenty-one centuries. He had no disciples to keep his name alive, yet in the twentieth century he had a feature film made of his life.

What did he do that people still remember him? Quite simply he was a slave who rebelled. He collected other slaves and fought back against his masters. He was from Thrace, an area bordering the Aegean Sea, stretching from the Danube to the Black Sea, now in the area of northern Greece, Bulgaria and Turkey. His fellow-gladiators comprised other Thracians, Gauls and Germans. Being sold as a gladiator was usually a form of punishment for a slave, but we are told that Spartacus and his colleagues were innocent of any crime.

We are also told he was brave, strong and intelligent, and his reported actions bear out his personal courage, his ability to lead others and his ingenuity in battle. Although a formidable enemy, he was also anathema to those in power at the time. Yet his memory withstood this hostility without any organised religion, hagiographer or biographer to bestow immortality on him. In the ancient world, he was an anti-hero. Typical of the ancient judgements is that of the Roman historian Florus:

One is able to endure even the shame of slaves in arms. For although slaves are persons who have been made subject to punishment in every possible way by some stroke of misfortune, they are still a type of human being, albeit an inferior type, and they are capable of being initiated into the benefits of the freedom that we enjoy. But I do not know what to call the war that was incited under the leadership of Spartacus. For when slaves served as soldiers and gladiators were their army commanders – the former the lowest sort of men, and the latter the worst – they simply added mockery to the disaster itself.

Spartacus' story is uncomplicated, though the aftermath of it is not. He was a slave who with a group of other gladiators fought their masters and won. They won spectacular victories against the mother of all armies, the Roman army. They held out against all the odds not for months but for years, in the very heart of the Roman Empire, Italy.

Wars against slaves were different from ordinary wars. When Romans killed slaves, they destroyed their own property and the loss was immense – although perhaps not as extreme as one author, Orosius, described when he wrote that 'the victors lost as much as the vanquished'. Victory was less satisfying but more necessary than against any other enemy. The Romans depended on their slaves; they were surrounded by them every minute of the day, their society could not run without them. Exact figures of slaves are beyond our grasp today, but we hear of some Romans possessing several hundred. An idea of the ubiquity of slaves is given by Julius Caesar who, when in a good mood, would give every man in his army a slave from Gaul. If all the slaves of Italy had joined Spartacus the decline and fall of the Roman Empire might have been much quicker. For the Romans it was a battle for life and death against Spartacus. Small wonder then that his name became a byword for monster.

Spartacus was not the only slave to rebel or to lead an army against his masters – for the Romans he was one in a series of such leaders. But Spartacus alone has caught the imagination of some very influential figures through the ages, not least Kirk Douglas, and he did this for a reason. He, perhaps uniquely, captures the essence of the underdog fighting back, the oppressed standing up to the oppressor. It is this simple act, this simple fact, which has done more than any other moral quality which he may have possessed.

In a way Spartacus is like Che Guevara, of whom most people have heard but about whom far fewer know very much. It is not important for them to know about him because he simply represents the idea of fighting back, or not being crushed. Whatever the truth of the historical Spartacus, he represents something powerful, something of immense potential for enormous numbers of people desperate for hope.

In this book I look at what we know about Spartacus from ancient writers and what later generations have made of this material. After a description of the outbreak of the revolt, there is a flashback in Chapter 2 which looks at how unusual (or not) such a rebellion was. The next two chapters follow the progress and end of the rebellion, and its aftermath is considered in Chapter 5. Chapter 6 is perhaps in one way the most significant since it is there that I examine how Spartacus came to have such a hold on the modern imagination, given that we know so little about him. Chapter 7 looks at three novels about Spartacus, all written in the twentieth century, which convey varying interpretations of what his story can teach us. Chapter 8 discusses the making of the famous film with Kirk Douglas, and the book ends with a few suggestions for further reading on different aspects of the topic.

In the interests of readability there are not many notes. This may upset some scholarly readers, but I hope I have given enough information for those interested to follow up any issues they wish. When I said I was writing this book, many colleagues looked on with puzzlement and pity. I want to thank Kieran Allen, John Curran, Jan Willem Drijvers, Roland Erne and Philip de Souza who took the time to read and comment on the text when they had much better things to do. The remaining errors and misjudgments are due to my own obstinacy. John Betts asked me if I would like to write this book and his invitation cheered me immensely. Deborah Blake has improved the text and allowed me to have Kirk Douglas on the cover. I dedicate the book to my grandfather because I think he might have liked it.

1

The Outbreak of Revolt

Spartacus was a gladiator in Capua in the first century BC at the time of the Roman Republic, before Rome had an emperor. In 73 BC he and some fellow-gladiators not only escaped from their masters, but even formed an army and took up arms against them. They succeeded for several years, travelling the length and breadth of Italy, fighting as true gladiators to the death.

Spartacus was a contemporary of Caesar, Cicero, Pompey and Crassus, the great names and great statesmen of Roman history. Rome had by this time won many wars and acquired an enormous Empire and great riches, not just from booty but also from taxes. Romans built roads, aqueducts, cities and sewers across their Empire, but those who were introduced to such civilisation paid for it with war and their blood.

The Roman Empire in 73 BC

In the mid-third century BC the Romans controlled only central and southern Italy. By the end of the first century BC they had subjugated most of the areas surrounding the Mediterranean Sea. Slaves, as well as loot, poured in from these wars of conquest, and individual Romans acquired wealth unheard of a century earlier. They used it to acquire yet more wealth, and to further their careers. It has been estimated that in the first century BC, at the time of the uprising of Spartacus, Italy had in the region of two million slaves out of a total population of perhaps six million.

Three hundred years or so earlier, the Greek philosopher Aristotle had suggested, sensibly from a slave-owner's point of view, a policy of divide and rule:

> If I am to state my own preference, the people who cultivate the land should be slaves; they should not all come from the same tribe or nation, and they should not be too courageous. This will make them useful workers and safe from the danger of revolt.

But the Romans grew careless in their good fortune and allowed many slaves from Syria to work the farms of Sicily. They paid for their carelessness. There were two major slave wars in Sicily in the sixty years before that led by Spartacus.

Traditionally Roman society had been divided into groups according to wealth. A man's social class depended on his role in the army, such was the importance of military matters in the life of the state. Political office was primarily concerned with military command over the citizens who served in the army. Every six years or so there was a census conducted of the citizen body of Rome, which was divided into five classes. The divisions were made solely on the basis of property, the bottom category consisting of those who possessed the smallest amount. Each category of citizen was expected to provide weapons for their role in the army, and the weapons an individual could afford determined his military role. Rome's armies were thus traditionally recruited from independent citizen landowners of modest means, who served for a brief period and then returned to their farms.

However, some people were not in any of the five classes. If citizens did not possess even the small amount that would have qualified them for the lowest class they were termed 'capite censi' – that is, enrolled by a head count – and they did not serve in the army.

Above even the highest class were the very wealthy. Senators were at the very top rank of society, and to be a senator a man had to have held public office, to have been a magistrate. Senators were drawn from the equestrian order, who were very wealthy, originally comprising those with enough money to furnish a horse and be in the cavalry.

At first, as we have seen, men without property were excluded from the army. Thus military service, because it was the duty of a citizen, could be seen as a privilege. However the property qualification was gradually reduced until, in 107 BC, the general Marius allowed those with no property to serve. The Roman army had found it more and more difficult to maintain its manpower at a high enough level for all its needs.

It had become more difficult to recruit sufficient numbers, not just because Rome's army was growing and needed on longer campaigns, but also because people were being driven off the land. As wealth flowed in to the centre, those who acquired it naturally bought land, the primary area of investment. Those who could, acquired more land, which led to fewer small-holdings, which in turn yielded fewer soldiers.

The mass eviction of the poor from the land by the rich was a factor in the political conflicts and civil wars of the last century of the Roman Republic. In 133 BC Tiberius Gracchus, a Roman aristocrat and tribune of the plebs, proposed the redistribution of the public land held illegally by the rich. He had seen that the numbers of land-owning peasantry were declining. He therefore proposed that the tradition be continued of distributing land, seized by Rome during the conquest of Italy, to the landless. Since much of this land had been appropriated by the nobility, there was strong opposition from them to this suggestion. Tiberius Gracchus was clubbed to death in a riot, but it seems to have been acknowledged that he had identified a serious problem, since some land was in fact distributed to poor citizens. In the first century BC, soldiers who had served with, and therefore had the patronage of, the great generals Sulla, Pompey and Julius Caesar, often received land at the end of their military service, but they usually took over farms already being cultivated by other smallholders.

The land bought up by the rich was often worked by slaves since they were so plentiful. Naturally many free poor families, who no longer had any land, fled to Rome, which by the end of the first century BC had perhaps one million inhabitants. This metropolis in turn was a huge market for food produced on Italian farms and in the provinces. Sicily in particular was an important source of wheat for Rome.

Rome's power did not increase unchecked. Just before the

gladiators' revolt, the Italians rebelled against the Roman domination of the Italian peninsula. From 91-87 BC Rome fought her own Italian allies and regained peace only by ceding citizenship to them. As Rome could not recruit enough Roman citizens for her military needs, allied troops were often used. But the Italians, although expected to provide an army to fight for Rome, had no say in political decisions. The Italians won their citizenship but, according to the historian Appian, resentment lingered on. He describes how the king of Pontus, Mithridates, an individual inimical to Rome, observed the attitude of the Italians to their powerful neighbour:

> He knew that almost all of Italy had recently revolted from the Romans because of the hatred the Italians had for them, that the Italians had fought a protracted war against the Romans, and that they had sided with the gladiator Spartacus against the Romans, even though he was a wholly disreputable person.

One reason why Spartacus and his army survived as long as they did was because the Italians were happy to allow Rome's enemy passage through their territory.

The gladiator in 73 BC

Another result of this new wealth enjoyed by the Romans was more conspicuous consumption. And it is difficult to imagine consumption more conspicuous in the ancient world than gladiatorial games, places where people and animals were slaughtered for entertainment. Great effort and thought, as well as money, were invested in this amusement, and there were centres known as schools (Latin *ludi*) where men, and sometimes women, were trained and maintained.

Capua was one such centre, situated about 125 miles south of Rome, just north-east of Naples. In 73 BC two hundred gladiators planned to escape from the gladiatorial school in Capua owned by Lentulus Batiatus, but, we are told, this first plan was betrayed. About seventy of the gladiators decided to go ahead despite this betrayal. Arming themselves with kitchen knives and cooking skewers, they succeeded in breaking out. Perhaps the original plan had involved better preparation, as kitchen utensils hardly seem adequate weapons against the soldiers used to guard these professional fighters. However luck was on the rebels' side. Once outside the school, they came across a wagon filled with gladiatorial weaponry and seized it, thus arming themselves more effectively, and headed south towards Mount Vesuvius. Once they reached the safety of a naturally well-protected spot, the haven of a volcano, Vesuvius, they elected three leaders, Crixus, Oenomaus and Spartacus.

The gladiators in the school, according to our main source, Plutarch, were mostly Gauls and Thracians, and there were also some Germans. Confusingly, these are also names for common types of gladiators, who fought in the national arms of typical Roman enemies. So what appears to be a label telling us where a man came from, may in fact be telling us what kind of armour he wore when he fought. For instance there is a tombstone of a gladiator which tells us that he was a Thracian, who fought as a Samnite. The Samnites were old enemies of the Romans, being a group of tribes in central and southern Apennines. Their armour was characterised by large rectangular shields, plumed helmets and short swords. Pliny the Elder also refers to a gladiator famous for his use of Samnite weapons, and it does seem that a gladiator's weapons did not necessarily reflect his origins. However here Plutarch clearly did regard these terms as ethnic labels, because a little later on he says that the gladiators were heading towards their homelands, Thrace and Gaul.

This group of fewer than a hundred men, Gauls and Thracians and Germans among them, escaped and defeated the soldiers who had immediately been sent out of Capua to retrieve them. The rebels not only defeated them but also seized their weapons, abandoning their gladiatorial swords and shields gladly as they preferred regular arms to these souvenirs of their previous existence.

The army of former gladiators became huge very quickly, perhaps as slaves heard of the outbreak but presumably also because they called on others to join them. Even free people threw in their lot with the rebels. They needed more and more weapons and started to arm themselves with clubs and daggers taken from travellers they met. They obtained food and provisions by raiding settlements. Spartacus, the overall leader according to the sources, divided all material gained from such raiding equally, which increased his and his army's popularity.

One Roman historian, Appian, relates the detail that Spartacus had been in the Roman army before being made a prisoner and sold as a slave. Another historian, Florus, elaborates on this a little more: that he had been a soldier, had deserted, had become a bandit and then a gladiator. Some therefore hold that this was where he learnt his soldiery – he had been in the Roman army and therefore had some idea of what was needed to counter it.

However, the skills of a gladiator were also very useful. In training them to fight for their lives, the Romans had done the gladiators a favour. They were accustomed to fighting to the death, in the knowledge that their only chance of survival was to win. The principle of fighting to victory or death was ingrained in them. They had no option to stop or surrender in the amphitheatre, and they remembered this lesson well in what happened next.

The games

It seems slightly strange that Romans did train their slaves to fight in this way. Surely training ones' underlings to be powerful, determined fighters ran the risk that they would turn their weapons against their oppressors? It is certainly true that after Spartacus, precautions were taken to make sure there was no other rebellion, although this did not extend to abandoning gladiatorial training. In fact, games became bigger and more lavish with greater and greater numbers of combatants. Julius Caesar recognised the importance of scale. In 65 BC he gave games for his dead father that involved six hundred and forty gladiators. Suetonius, who wrote a biography of Caesar, describes typical events which he hosted as consisting of the following:

1. The Outbreak of Revolt

Wild-beast hunts took place five days running, and the entertainment ended with a battle between two armies, each consisting of five hundred infantry, twenty elephants and thirty cavalry .... The naval battle was fought on an artificial lake dug in the Lesser Codeta, between Tyrian and Egyptian ships, with two, three, or four banks of oars, and heavily manned.

Gladiators were usually defeated enemies or slaves who had committed an offence. Going to gladiatorial schools was a punishment, though Plutarch tells us specifically that Spartacus and his men had been sent to the school even though they had committed no offence. In other words, they were wrongly condemned and their moral outrage may have lent fervour to their fighting. We do also hear of free men voluntarily becoming gladiators, but these cases are mentioned because they are unusual. The vast majority would have been slaves. And their status was the lowest, since they were slaves who had done something wrong and whose chances of dying in the near future were very high.

Hand-to-hand combat was not something as removed from everyday life in ancient Rome as it is for most people today. All Roman males would have been soldiers at some time and therefore knew what fighting was. They respected skill in combat. Thus successful gladiators could earn some fame and popularity even if they had no legal rights at all. Good fighters were popular favourites, celebrities even, like successful racehorses today. And as with racehorses, winners were loved and deaths might be regretted, but it was all part of the sport.

Such games had first been put on at funerals, as a form of respect. One might even describe it as a variety of human sacrifice. The first games at Rome were at the funeral of an aristocrat in the mid-third century BC, whose sons had three pairs of gladiators fight to the death. The fashion caught on. In 216 BC Marcus Aemilius Lepidus' funeral had twenty-two pairs of gladiators, in 200 BC at another funeral there were twenty-five, in 183 there were sixty pairs.

Games became more elaborate and lasted longer. In order to impress greater variety was introduced and there are lists of barbarians paraded for the Roman populace – Blemmyans, Germans, Sarmatians, Isaurians, Exomites, Yemenites, Indians, Bactrians, Iberians, Saracens, Persians, Goths, Alans, Roxalani, Franks, Suabians, Vandals, Palmyrenes. Such variety also meant that few would have had a common language making organisation difficult.

Women gladiators and wild animals were introduced to spice things up a little. Under the emperors, a full programme of activities might include gladiatorial fights, executions of criminals and a wild beast hunt. A phenomenal variety of exotic animals was seen in the amphitheatre. Lions and leopards were first displayed and slaughtered in 186 BC, according to the historian Livy. Pompey when consul in 55 BC had twenty elephants, six hundred lions, four hundred and ten leopards, apes, a lynx and a rhinoceros. Caesar in 46 BC managed a giraffe. Later games included crocodiles, hyenas, hippopotamuses, ostriches, wild asses, stags, elks, gazelles, ibexes. What did they do with all the carcasses? Ate them perhaps, and threw the human corpses in the river.

1. The Outbreak of Revolt

Once Rome had an emperor, the games were strictly super-vised so that individuals other than the emperor should not get too popular. Augustus, the first emperor, set the tone. His games saw the deaths of four hundred and twenty leopards, dozens of elephants and up to four hundred bears and three hundred lions. In his *Res Gestae*, the autobiography he had inscribed on his mausoleum, he boasted that in his games ten thousand glad-iators fought in eight shows and that three and a half thousand animals died in twenty-six hours of his reign. The emperor Claudius held a sea-battle on the Fucine Lake in AD 52, and Tacitus says nineteen thousand criminals lost their lives in the spectacle. Sea-battles were also held in theatres which were flooded for the event. Titus, emperor for only two years, AD 79-81, put on games lasting a hundred days; these included the slaughter of nine thousand animals in one day. We must allow for some exaggeration, but even so what we see here is a cele-bration of violent death on an enormous scale.

Animals and slaves served a similar purpose in the Roman display. Both slaves, in their 'barbarian' arms, and animals repre-sent the natural world that the Romans control, and one might say, destroy. The whole attitude of the Romans towards the games has made modern scholars wince and waste much ink in an attempt to explain it. Yet there is perhaps less difference between this entertainment and the serious business of politics than one might think. The description by the Roman historian Tacitus of his countrymen, which he puts into the mouth of an ancient Briton, could describe the thirst for exotic animals and ever larger numbers of humans for the arena:

They plunder the whole world: and having exhausted the land, they now scour the sea. If their victims are rich, their greed is for gain; if they are poor, it is for glory; and neither East nor West can satisfy them. They are the only people in the world who covet wealth and want with equal greed. To robbery, murder, and pillage they give the false name of Empire, and when they make a wilderness they call it Peace.

Games were still being put on ten times a year in the fourth century AD, when the emperors were professed Christians. The bishops did not approve.

Gladiators fought in places apart from Rome, although the larger the centre, the larger the games. Rome always outshone the rest of the Empire in the extravagance of her entertainment (the Colosseum in Rome seated about fifty thousand). Sometimes putting on games for the public was part of a magistrate's duties. Most gladiatorial shows in small towns were not voluntary but produced by leading citizens as a tax on status, an obligation but also an opportunity for self-enhancement.

Options for gladiators

Life was grim for the gladiator. Some preferred death, even achieved in what most would consider extremely unpleasant ways. According to Seneca,

> The following incident happened recently in a school that trains beast fighters. While one of the Germans was engaged in a training session for the morning spectacles, he went off to

relieve himself. No other opportunity was ever allowed to him to have an unguarded moment of privacy. In the latrine, he picked up the stick tipped with a sponge which was provided for the purposes of cleaning one's obscene parts [the Roman equivalent of toilet paper]. Then, jamming the whole thing down his throat, he blocked his windpipe and suffocated himself to death.

Seneca goes on to describe another suicide in which a gladiator, on his way to the amphitheatre, stuck his head in the moving spokes of a cart, which snapped his neck.

After the second Sicilian slave war, the survivors of the rebel army were taken to Rome to fight wild beasts, but they were rebellious to the end and refused to fight. Instead they killed each other and the last man left killed himself.

In the fourth century AD, more than four hundred years after Spartacus, Symmachus described disgustedly in a letter to his brother how some Saxon gladiators had strangled themselves rather than fight in the amphitheatre:

How indeed could the best private security have stopped the impious hands of such a desperate group of men?

They were impious because they killed themselves and spoiled Symmachus' show. He remarks that wild animals would have been better than this gang of slaves 'worse than Spartacus himself'. So the memory of Spartacus was alive and well years after his death.

It is customary to think of Romans falling honourably on their swords, but this had not always been acceptable. Before Stoics taught that 'the door is always open' (i.e. you always have the option to kill yourself), suicide was seen as sinful by some Romans and, bizarre to modern eyes, although perhaps not to medieval Christians, could be punished by crucifixion. Pliny the Elder tells us that Tarquinius Priscus, an early king of Rome, had punished those who committed suicide to avoid work on the sewers by crucifying their corpses, so that their fellow-citizens would see their bodies rotting and being torn to pieces by animals.

It is not difficult to see why some gladiators might wish to escape their school. However, Spartacus' aims have been endlessly discussed. In Soviet historiography, huge claims were made for this slave-leader, which Western scholars were keen to refute. Joseph Vogt set the tone:

> The brave undertaking of the slaves has about it a touch of the tragedy of any attempt to achieve the impossible.[1]

Keith Bradley tells us:

> It becomes impossible to view the Spartacan movement as being in any way dominated by abstract or ideological imperatives: freedom from slavery was the intent of the fugitives; the slavery system itself remained unaffected.[2]

Thomas Wiedemann remarks:

> Spartacus' slave rebellion has become a symbol of 'proletarian' resistance to oppression .... The leaders were Celts, Germans

and Thracians, and unlike the Sicilian slaves their objective (insofar as it was not simply to plunder Italy) was not to set up a Hellenistic monarchy, but to return to their tribal homelands.[3]

J.G. Griffith begins an article on Spartacus with the comment:

Spartacus is an attractive figure, especially to Englishmen, who have a congenital fondness for a gallant loser ... yet authoritative works in English, the fruits of a long tradition of rigorous historical criticism, say little about him.[4]

He goes on to ask whether his Oxford tutors were right to dismiss Spartacus as insignificant. And, perhaps unsurprisingly, answers yes. Spartacus was a minor figure, ignored by most of our sources and ignored by sensible modern scholars.

It is uncontroversial to agree that Spartacus wanted to be free. He did not have to be hugely intelligent to see that he would have a greater chance of surviving by fighting alongside his colleagues instead of against them. If caught, he and they knew they would be killed. But even if they won several fights in the arena, they knew they would die sooner or later.

Aims of the slave army

So Spartacus was fighting to escape the life of a gladiator, but he was more than a fugitive. Others must have broken out and fled singly or in groups. This large group is unusual in deciding to fight. Similar episodes have happened in modern history, and the phenomenon of groups of ex-slaves living an independent existence has been well documented. It seems, however, that Spartacus' group was not simply trying to find a niche in which they could survive. The army soon became too big for this to be feasible or tolerable in any sense for the Romans. It would have been counterproductive to collect thousands of followers if they were trying to run away. Groups split up if they want to escape. Some of the historians of the day tell us that Spartacus' men made declarations to groups of slaves, that they were encouraging others to join them as well as merely attracting followers. After a while their success must have had its own momentum, but at first they seem to have been out to recruit, not to flee.

It may have been that they saw their only options as victory or death. Maybe that stark choice was how they saw the world and their fate. To win they needed *all* the slaves in Italy. This may not have looked so unrealistic to them as it does to us, since slave revolts did not usually happen in isolation. Slaves heard of outbreaks, such as the great wars in Sicily, and even though these ended in the deaths of the participants and so might be described as having failed, they succeeded in sparking off new revolts.

In the period leading up to Spartacus' revolt, there had been an enormous increase in wealth in the Roman Empire, including a massive increase in slavery. Perhaps unsurprisingly, this caused unforeseen problems. However, by the time of Spartacus, after two damaging slave wars in Sicily, one must assume that the Romans had learnt their lesson – although perhaps Lentulus Batiatus, the owner of the gladiatorial school in Capua, may have been a little careless. We do not know the exact ethnic make-up of the seventy or so followers of Spartacus, except that they included Gauls, Germans and Thracians, but they must had some language in common, probably Latin. Given the actions of the rebel army, it is clear that they were aiming for something more than suicide or flight.

As Synesius, a fifth-century bishop, said many years later:

The followers of Spartacus and Crixus were not from the same country as their leaders, nor were they of the same nation, and only their common lot and their fate drew them together for the campaign. And this is only natural. For I believe every slave to be the enemy of his master when it appears possible to over-power him.

2

Previous Revolts

Spartacus was not the only rebel slave-leader in antiquity, but he is the most famous. This has a tendency to distort our view of the past. Since Spartacus' rebellion is the best known, and since it lasted more than two years or so, one might assume that others were less impressive, being shorter and smaller in scale. But fame does not necessarily indicate success even though fame itself is some sort of success. In fact slave revolts were more common than one might think, and although the evidence is scanty we have enough to know that there were such revolts that were more successful on all counts than that of Spartacus.

Arguably the greatest loss from the ancient world is a history of the slave wars by someone called Caecilius from Kale Akte in Sicily. We know of this text from another writer, but no manuscript of the work has survived. It is more than probable that we do not have information about most of the revolts, and much of the information we do have is brief in the extreme. But we do have enough clues to know that there were others.

2. Previous Revolts

The Greek world

In the classical Greek period, the slaves in Sparta called helots were constantly rebelling. Sometimes they are distinguished from slaves in modern writing because although they were not free they belonged to the land rather than to individuals. However ancient writers themselves frequently referred to them as slaves since the crucial criterion for them was the helots' lack of freedom. Helots differed from most other unfree populations in speaking a common language and sharing a common heritage. The helots were the original inhabitants of certain places in the Peloponnese, such as Messenia, whom the Dorians had enslaved. They were a constant source of stress for the Spartans since they took every opportunity to rebel. In the fourth century BC, when the Peloponnese was invaded by a Theban army, the Messenians eventually won their freedom. This victory should be termed a successful slave revolt, although it rarely is.

Another uprising which we know about from the Greek world occurred on the island of Chios and seems to have taken place in the third century BC. It involved what today is called a maroon community, that is the slaves formed a permanent and autonomous group. Slaves had been running away in large numbers, forming bases in hills and attacking masters' houses. They formed a coherent group under a leader with authority, called Drimakos. Under him, the slaves resisted forces sent out against them. Drimakos persuaded the Chians to accept a treaty. He was able to do this because the owners could not win. Under the treaty he agreed that the slaves would not steal more than a certain amount and that he would only accept as recruits those who had been very badly treated. We are told that when the slaves realised that Drimakos kept his word, they ran away less often to join him because they knew that to be accepted they would have satisfy him as to their ill-treatment by their owners.

Drimakos thus made an accommodation with the owners. His men did not steal too much and they did not foment revolution. And the treaty was kept until Drimakos grew old. However, even though the owners agreed to this arrangement, they constantly promised a reward for his capture or his head, the prize being a large sum of money and freedom. It is a tribute to Drimakos' achievement that no one claimed the prize. One must assume that his followers felt they had achieved freedom; in any case they were loyal to him. But when Drimakos grew old he told his lover to decapitate him and claim the money for his head. His boyfriend, presumably overcoming some reluctance, carried out this suggestion, exchanged Drimakos' head for the money and left for his own country.

The aim of this group appears to have been escape from slavery for themselves, and this they achieved. They did not carry on continual warfare against their former masters nor seek to control the whole island. Instead they survived free and in a relatively stable situation, but only while Drimakos lived. After his death, there was uncontrolled ravaging by runaways. Chian landowners as well as slaves looked back with nostalgia to the old days when there was some order on the island. Unsurprisingly, runaway slaves dedicated the first-fruits of everything they stole to the memory of Drimakos. More bizarrely, they brought these gifts to a shrine of the Kindly Hero erected, *by the land-owners*, to Drimakos. Both sides claimed him as their benefactor, although he would seem to have favoured his old enemies more since he was said to appear to Chians in their sleep and warn them when their slaves were plotting against them.

The Roman world

Rome had had trouble with slave revolts long before Spartacus, though our evidence for early Roman history is not copious. Livy records that uprisings occurred at Setia and Praeneste just south of Rome in 198 BC, after great numbers of slaves came to Italy after the second war against Carthage at the end of the third century BC. These slaves approached other slaves in the neighbouring areas to join their revolt. The plot was betrayed and an army of nearly two thousand men arrested the leaders while many slaves fled. Five hundred were arrested and executed at Praeneste, and in Rome much greater care was thereafter taken of the prisoners of war, in the shape of heavy leg-irons.

But slaves continued to take their chances, and Livy reports that two years later there was a rebellion in Etruria. One constant feature of slave revolts is that regardless of their success or failure, uprisings inspired others elsewhere to have a go. Although our records are brief, the trouble seems to have been of great consequence to the Romans, who spent much effort quelling these rebellions. Ten years later there was an uprising in Apulia, again in southern Italy, resulting in the condemnation of seven thousand slaves. Although many escaped, comments Livy, many were punished. We do not know the duration of these uprisings or how many were involved, but this ignorance should not lead us to assume automatically that the threat was negligible or less than that posed by the two Sicilian slave wars, about which, by chance, we know rather more. We also find that whenever the status quo was threatened, the threatening side is often accused of recruiting the help of slaves for their nefarious purposes. This may be true, or it may reflect the perceived truth in the saying *quot servi, tot hostes* – 'all slaves are enemies'.

More important for Spartacus was that there had been two major slave wars within living memory, the last one ending only thirty years before his uprising. Interestingly, one ancient writer tells us that Spartacus had the idea of sending two thousand men over to take the island of Sicily, rekindling the great conflict on the island which had only recently been controlled. The two Sicilian wars lasted several years each, and unlike the original followers of Spartacus, the slaves who took part in these wars were not professional soldiers but herdsmen and farmhands.

The first Sicilian slave war

All of them donned the most powerful weapon of all: a rage that was directed at the destruction of their arrogant and overbearing masters.

So writes Diodorus Siculus as he gives an account of the outbreak of the first Sicilian slave war. Our knowledge of the two wars, though not copious, is much fuller than for any previous uprisings. This is thanks to this writer from Sicily, Diodorus, whose importance in a history of ancient slavery is immense. Not only did he detail the events, which in itself shows some sympathy, but he also presented the slaves as victims of injustice in a manner very unusual for ancient writers. He lived after the events he described, in the first century BC, and in fact the relevant books of his large history of the world have not survived, so that all that remains of those covering the slave wars are summaries from other writers. Nevertheless this is much more than we normally possess on such topics, so that for once we can read more than a couple of sentences about a slave revolt.

The exact dates of the first war are not known, but even conservative estimates have given five years for its duration, which is a very long time for a revolt. Possible starting dates are as early as the 140s BC. It is generally agreed to have finished in 132. Some details are less shaky.

Vast numbers of slaves had been imported into Sicily, the first Roman province, after Rome's successes in the eastern Mediterranean in the first half of the second century BC. Many came from Syria, so that they had a common language and culture and relative freedom to communicate with each other while they worked the land or looked after the animals. There were so many that their masters did not, or perhaps could not, provide for them properly. The slaves therefore, in order to feed and clothe themselves, turned to mugging travellers. Soon they controlled most of the roads of Sicily, striking fear into the authorities.

One particular Sicilian couple were such cruel owners that

their slaves plotted revenge, seeking help from a fellow-slave who was reputed to have supernatural abilities. This man was called Eunus and he impressed his fellows not only by the co-incidence of his name, which means 'well-disposed' or 'friendly' in Greek, but also by apparently performing miracles. This wonder-worker claimed to be in contact with a Syrian goddess.

Eunus' advice about revolt was that the slaves should go ahead, as long as they did so immediately. They followed his advice and were immensely successful. They broke open barracks, setting free the slaves who were imprisoned there at night, and took the city of Enna. They declared Eunus their king, and he changed his name to Antiochus, reflecting the Syrian origins of many of the slaves. Antiochus was the name of several Seleucid kings of Syria, so the envisaged structure of the new order seems to have been based on one with which the slaves were already familiar. The slaves killed their masters, except those who could make weapons, and these they set to work. The Roman forces sent out to take charge were easily beaten off because the slaves had such vast numbers – one source tells us ten thousand – in their army.

At roughly the same time, in another part of the island near Agrigentum, Cleon, who was from Cilicia, a place which became famous for its pirates, led another revolt. This too was successful and the slaves took the city of Agrigentum. Cleon and Eunus/Antiochus joined forces, thus becoming enormously powerful. Cleon seems to have happily taken the subordinate role. The slaves took several cities in Sicily and in practice controlled the island, to the horror of the Romans. They defeated several Roman armies sent out against them (led by praetorian prefects and two consuls) and their numbers increased to two hundred thousand.

In 132 BC a third consul was sent out. He persuaded a slave to betray his colleagues, and this single act of betrayal allowed the Romans to retake Enna and Tauromenium, the main centres of resistance. The slave king Eunus/Antiochus was arrested and died the wretched death of being consumed by worms in prison. It was said that more than twenty thousand slaves were killed at the end of the war. Any rebel found alive was crucified.

The slave army does not seem to have had as one of its aims escape or return to Syria. It stayed in Sicily and fought there for several years. There was a clear hierarchical structure and if the slaves had succeeded, it seems that they would have established a monarchy along Seleucid lines. Ultimately they did not succeed and the Romans did their best to discourage others from following their example. In fact, slaves seized the moment and revolted in several places in Italy, Athens and Delos, but these uprisings were crushed immediately.

Trouble in Pergamum

Overlapping with this war was a revolt in Asia Minor by a man called Aristonicus after the death of king Attalus III. The Romans laid claim to his kingdom after the king's death in 133, arguing that he had bequeathed it to them. Aristonicus, the illegitimate son of Attalus' father, so a half-brother of the king, seized the kingdom and held out against the Romans until 129 BC.

His army was described as consisting of the lower classes, slaves and non-Greeks, which could reflect abuse from historians sympathetic to the Romans, or desperation on the part of Aristonicus. Nevertheless the curious detail is recorded that the large group of the poor and slaves which he assembled were called *Heliopolitae* 'Citizens of the Sun', which implies that there were some idealistic aims behind the uprising of establishing a utopia, a city of the Sun. Although the aim of Aristonicus was to establish himself as heir to Attalus, he drew on the discontent of slaves for his support. The slaves seized their opportunity and so did he and in a way this uprising looks very similar to those in Sicily, although the leader was not a slave. Diodorus, in the course of describing the first slave war, describes the events in Asia Minor thus:

> Almost the identical thing happened in Asia at this time, when Aristonicus claimed the kingship that was not rightly his. Because their masters had treated them so terribly, the slaves in Asia joined Aristonicus and were the cause of great disasters to many unfortunate cities.

The second Sicilian slave war

The second war lasted for four years and the dates are more certain than for the previous one, being generally accepted as approximately 104-100 BC. The inspiration of slave revolts should not be underestimated. Shortly before the second slave war, there were three small uprisings, all in Italy. The first was at Nuceria and was crushed almost as it started; the second at Capua, where two hundred slaves rebelled.

The third was led by a young man of equestrian rank, Titus Vettius Minutius, who fell foul of his creditors. Diodorus gives us some details which confuse rather than clarify the story. Apparently Vettius Minutius fell in love with a slave girl. He wished to buy her but could not afford her. He armed four hundred of his own slaves, beheaded his creditors and soon acquired a following of more than three and a half thousand slaves. The praetor sent out to deal with him, perhaps learning from the end of the first slave war, bribed one of the rebel commanders. The Romans made the most of their advantage and the rebels, seeing all was lost, cut their own throats.

Clearly there are a few problems with this story. If the young man owned four hundred slaves how could he not have been able to afford the woman with whom he was infatuated? But this is how we are told the story by our source, Diodorus. We learn also that there was a rebellion in the mines of Athens at the same time as the second slave war, that there were many of these slave rebellions, and that large numbers of slaves were killed in all of them.

The second Sicilian slave war had a specific cause, although presumably the rebels also took courage from these three previous revolts. The Roman general, Marius, needed more troops to help him against the tribe of the Cimbri. He asked Nicomedes, king of Bithynia, to send him troops. However, Nicomedes replied that he could not comply because most of his countrymen had been enslaved by Roman government contractors. This improbable reply was not taken as a joke but rather seems to have had a basis in reality. A law was then passed saying that no free citizen of an allied state could be enslaved in a Roman province. If it was found that any had been, the governors of the provinces were to set them free.

As a consequence of this law the governor of Sicily, Licinius Nerva, freed about eight hundred slaves before the local landowners started to protest, urging him to stop, since they objected to seeing their property simply walk off. However by this time many slaves had come to the main city of Sicily, Syracuse, to seek their freedom. When the governor ordered them back to their masters, they decided to take action. Some formed a group and ran off. Their numbers escalated and the governor was unable to quell them, so he persuaded a bandit to betray them. The rebels welcomed this bandit, believing him to be their friend, even going so far as to make him one of their commanders. He betrayed them, and those who were not killed fighting the Romans threw themselves off a cliff. The rebellion seemed to have failed.

However, a report came in that eighty more slaves had killed their master. Because he had already disbanded his army, the governor did not take swift enough action. The slaves mocked him as a coward, incited more to join them and within seven days had gathered and armed more than eight hundred men. Soon after this they numbered six thousand.

As in the first revolt, the slaves elected a king, this time called Salvius. Again the aim seems to have been to achieve a monarchical structure. This is not surprising, but modern scholars have been quick to assert that there is no abolitionist movement here, nor any revolutionary one either since the systems the slaves would have put in place were simply the ones with which they were already familiar. Like Eunus, Salvius was a man with religious connections – he made prophecies and played the flute at women's religious festivals. Despite such rather unfavourable details, Salvius seems to have been austere, ordering his men to avoid cities since they were sources of laziness and excess. He trained and organised them efficiently and soon they have acquired enough equipment to field two thousand cavalry and twenty thousand infantry.

Their next move was to attack Morgantina. The Roman governor Nerva and ten thousand soldiers marched to meet them and captured their camp, which was empty and only lightly guarded. The slaves however returned and attacked. The Roman army started to run away. Salvius made a declaration that if they threw down their arms they would not be killed. Astonishingly – at least astonishingly for Roman historians – most of the Roman soldiers complied, and Salvius retook his camp. Because of this humane proclamation only six hundred of the Roman army died, while four thousand were taken prisoner.

After this success, Salvius doubled his army and tried to take Morgantina again. He promised freedom to all the slaves in the city, but their masters promised the same if they defended it. The slaves trusted their masters, mistakenly, and when the governor later rescinded these grants of freedom, most of the slaves ran away and joined the rebels.

In another part of the island around Segesta and Lilybaeum, there was another revolt led by Athenion, a Cilician, again another detail similar to the last war. He also was reputed to be skilled in predicting the future (the gods told him, among other things, that he would be king of Sicily) and persuaded two hundred slaves who worked with him to join him. He then recruited slaves on neighbouring farms until he had more than a thousand with him within five days.

Once king, Salvius, like Eunus, changed his name, this time to Tryphon, and contacted Athenion, who, in a situation very similar to the first war, became Tryphon's general. Much is made of the adoption of royal names but it could be that both Eunus and Salvius were reverting to their real names. Salvius/Tryphon built himself a marketplace and palace at Triokala, appointed intelligent people to be his advisers, wore a purple Roman toga and Greek cloak, and was escorted by lictors bearing fasces, the symbols of Roman power.

The Roman Senate in the meantime sent out a praetor with seventeen thousand men. They defeated the slaves, killing twenty thousand and wounding Athenion. The survivors were understandably demoralised. The Romans besieged Triokala but then withdrew. When Tryphon died, Athenion took over and reigned successfully while the Romans apparently did nothing.

Finally, the Senate in 101 BC sent out a consul, who succeeded where so many commanders had failed. He fought a duel with Athenion and killed him. Although the consul was wounded himself he carried on to fight the remaining ten thousand slaves and eventually defeated them. About a thousand slaves surrendered and were taken to Rome to fight as gladiators. However, when they realised that this was what was in store for them, they killed each other and the last man killed himself.

These events in Sicily were very damaging to Rome. The repercussions were felt on the mainland and beyond. Both lasted several years and encouraged slaves elsewhere to throw off their chains. In both cases, kings were elected who modelled themselves on Hellenistic monarchs. There was no evidence of any attempt at social revolution or the abolition of slavery, and the participants appear to have had only personal freedom as their goal. Many scholars, admittedly in reaction to improbable claims for the revolutionary nature of such uprisings, have stressed this aspect, as if it undermined the importance of these events.

On the other hand, it ought to be borne in mind that most revolutions do not start out as such. If there were a call to change the world, a common reaction would be (and has been) to ignore it as it seems such a huge, impossible task. Small steps to progress are much more acceptable. Secondly, most people rebel because of immediate and concrete concerns, rather than for ideals. Even the Russian Revolution of 1917 started out demanding bread, peace and land rather than Socialism. Thirdly, monarchs sometimes can personify the identity of a group of people who identify with what they see as their own leader, preferable to imposed masters.

This emphasis on the conservative nature of the aims of slaves in revolt colours views of Spartacus, in that it is assumed Spartacus too lacked any bolder plan, and would simply have wanted to establish a system he already knew rather than create something different. While noting that Toussaint L'Ouverture, leader of the successful slave rebellion in the eighteenth century in Saint Domingue, also did not start out with the aim of the abolition of slavery but nevertheless arrived there after having started his fight for freedom, it should be observed that Spartacus' revolt was different from the Sicilian ones. He never declared himself king, so it is rather presumptuous to assume that that is what he wanted to be.

3

The First Victories

During the sixty years before Spartacus' revolt, the Roman world had been shaken by two serious slave rebellions which had each lasted several years and had to be quelled by consular armies. The vast numbers of slaves imported from the eastern Mediterranean to the island of Sicily must have helped organisation and communication in the rebel forces. Spartacus' forces were much less uniform and the circumstances of his breakout rather different from events in Sicily. He started out with very small numbers, although like most of the known events of his life, the sources do not agree on the details. Cicero, for instance, one of the very few contemporaries of Spartacus whose words about him survive, says that he had fewer than fifty men when he started out; a later writer, Florus, says that he only had thirty.

However, Appian and Plutarch, who give the fullest accounts of Spartacus that have survived, say that the figure was in the seventies. Appian gives Spartacus a bigger role in the early stages and says that he persuaded his fellow-gladiators to break out. In Plutarch's account, on the other hand, Spartacus grows into his role: the men escape, reach some form of safety and then choose three leaders for themselves, one of whom is Spartacus.

Plutarch tells us that one of the people who escaped with

Spartacus was his wife, a woman from his own tribe who was a prophetess and follower of Dionysus. No more is heard of her, and she is only mentioned by Plutarch once because she interpreted the snake which coiled up round Spartacus' face while he slept. As seen earlier, we do not know what she thought it signified, nor what Plutarch said she thought it signified, because the manuscripts differ about a word.

First Spartacus and his men defeated the soldiers who had pursued them out of Capua. They seized these soldiers' weapons and threw away their gladiatorial arms, because they saw the latter as dishonourable and barbaric. The progression of the type of weapons is interesting: the rebels started out with kitchen equipment, which one might say was used by slave women, the lowest possible category. Then they acquired gladiatorial arms, which was a step up but still with unpleasant associations of servitude. Finally, however, they gained control of the weapons of the Roman soldiers they had defeated. From this moment, they were fighting on equal terms with their enemies. On the other hand, if we remember Diodorus as he described the Sicilian war, they were from the beginning in possession of the most powerful weapon of all – rage.

The praetor Gaius Claudius Glaber

The Romans then sent out a praetor, Gaius Claudius Glaber, with three thousand men. Praetors were magistrates who could perform almost all the activities of a consul, the highest position in the state, and indeed they were the main magistrates in Rome if the consuls were absent. The fact that a praetor was sent out immediately against Spartacus shows that the Romans took the threat seriously. Glaber and his army besieged the gladiators, who had installed themselves on Mount Vesuvius, twenty miles or so south of Capua.

This refuge, although a suitable metaphor for the sudden explosion of the Roman underclass, was not as perilous as it might seem to modern readers for whom this volcano is famous for devastating Pompeii and Herculaneum. In fact at the time of its eruption in AD 79 it had not erupted for more than seven centuries. More than four thousand feet high, it rises above the Bay of Naples and the western base rests almost on the shore. After the first two thousand feet there is a high, semi-circular ridge called Mount Somma, and it is thought that Spartacus and his men camped here, surrounded by rocks covered by wild vines. The earth surrounding this area is very fertile, and modern Vesuvius is covered with vineyards and orchards.

There was only one narrow path up to the ridge and this was guarded by the Roman army. The rest of the mountain was sheer rock, affording neither access nor exit – at least at first sight. For a while it must have seemed as if the slave army had taken refuge in a dead end. The Romans assumed that eventually, when food and water gave out, the gladiators would be forced down the path. They therefore encamped at the bottom of the mountain, unhurriedly, confident in their fighting ability, organisation, equipment – in other words, all the professional accoutrements of the greatest army the world had ever seen. They were after all only rounding up local runaway slaves, a motley gang of rebels who seemed to have voluntarily backed themselves into a corner.

However, necessity is the mother of invention, and the slaves came up with a cunning plan. They cut the wild vines, which grew so luxuriantly around them, and wove them into what must have been extremely long ladders that could take them all the way to the foot of the mountain. They all climbed safely down these ladders, with the last man throwing down the weapons and then abseiling down himself. In this way they had the advantage of total surprise. They surrounded the besieging army, attacked them suddenly and put them to flight. According to one source, Frontinus, this masterpiece of resourcefulness, imagination and physical courage was carried out by only the seventy-four original gladiators. That is, by themselves they put to flight all the Roman cohorts. If this is what happened, it was an incredible feat. Certainly the gladiators had more adherents after this victory, as herdsmen and shepherds threw in their lot with them. They victorious rebels seized the Roman camp with all its possessions and supplies.

Even if their numbers had expanded before this point, the rebels had won by brain power rather than strength in numbers. And this surprise tactic must have been humiliating for the Romans, who had felt assured of easy victory. At the time, this eruption of men was as unexpected as the more conventional type of volcanic action. From breaking out with some kitchen knives, the gladiators defeated the troops sent out to recover them, fled to a natural safe haven, and by sheer ingenuity and daring – the two main characteristics of the Spartacan revolt – put the Roman army to flight.

The praetor Publius Varinius

The next disaster for the Romans took place when they sent another praetor, Publius Varinius, with more Roman forces, plus two subordinates, Furius and Cossinius. Unfortunately Appian and Plutarch, our two major sources, give us very few details about the engagements that followed except to say that the rebels overcame them with ease several times.

Furius, who had two thousand men with him, was defeated by the rebel army without any trouble. Spartacus almost captured Cossinius when the latter was bathing at Salinae. This vignette of the Roman at ease being surprised by rebel daring is in Plutarch's account, and he may have taken it from Sallust, as fragments of the latter's work mention Cossinius washing himself in a spring belonging to a villa nearby. The Romans were again taken off their guard, illustrating what the Romans themselves later thought characterised this whole debacle for them: their own carelessness and the ingenuity of the slave-leader. Cossinius escaped this humiliation with difficulty but was pursued and killed a short while later in an engagement over his own camp, which Spartacus captured, taking the supplies.

Sallust, writing in the first century BC and thus much closer in time to Spartacus than Plutarch and Appian, wrote an account of Spartacus' revolt. Although work survives in only a fragmentary state, there are some coherent details. Sallust tells us that the soldiers who had been defeated and ran away did not return to their units and that some of the rest of the men were refusing to fight. However Varinius had four thousand men still willing to do their duty and so he ordered a camp to be set up, fortified with walls and a moat, near the rebel encampment.

Knowing when to avoid open conflict, the slaves decided to retreat. Because the Romans were so close they had to do so secretly. Usually at night-time their camp was guarded by watchmen and soldiers, so to keep up as normal an appearance as possible the next night they left a solitary signalman in place, lit many fires, dressed up fresh corpses and tied them to stakes so that from a distance the Romans would think they were still there, and then quietly left. The Romans were indeed fooled and only noticed something was wrong when they missed the customary insults shouted across at them, and the bombardment of stones that normally woke them in the morning. The rebels had safely slipped off into the night.

There were several more engagements with the praetor Varinius, but again accounts are brief in the extreme and we learn merely that the Romans lost them all. The final disgrace was when the slaves captured the Roman lictors and even Varinius' own horse. The symbolism of the horse is clear: the mighty animal subdued by the Romans, made to work their will and carry them across their Empire, is taken over by ex-slaves.

Lictors were the attendants who carried the fasces for magistrates. They accompanied them at all times inside and outside Rome, proceeding before them in a single file, each carrying the fasces on his left shoulder. Consuls had twelve lictors and praetors had six. The fasces were bundles of wooden rods approximately five feet long and a single-headed axe, all held together with a red thong. They were the expression of magisterial authority and were regarded as instruments of execution. For slaves to gain possession of them would have caused apoplexy at Rome.

Plutarch says that it was after this point that Spartacus became a figure of fame and fear. To have defeated one praetor might have been interpreted as luck, or a Roman army that was not concentrating hard enough. Two defeats put Spartacus and his army into a different category of enemy, and the next time the Senate sent out two legions with two consuls. They could not take him more seriously. As Plutarch says,

> Because of the fear and the danger of the situation they [the Senate] dispatched both consuls together to the war, much as they would send consuls to a regular war of the greatest difficulty and magnitude.

Not only was the danger great, but the humiliation must have made the pain worse; to send out a Roman army against their own slaves meant treating them as equals.

The consuls

After this victory, slaves flocked to join the insurgents. Although exact figures are impossible and all the sources differ, one says that after this point Spartacus' army numbered seventy thousand, which if true meant that they vastly outnumbered the forces, fewer than ten thousand men, sent out against them. The fact that Spartacus and his commanders were able to arm and feed even half this number is impressive in itself.

The two consuls for 72 BC were Lucius Gellius Publicola and Gnaeus Cornelius Lentulus. They were sent out against this burgeoning rebel army with two legions. Legions consisted of ten cohorts, which in turn comprised six centuries. There were, confusingly, only eighty men in a century, so a legion comprised four thousand eight hundred men in total.

Again the ancient accounts contain very few specific details. Plutarch says that after the victory over Varinius, Spartacus headed north and the new Roman force defeated the Germans who had separated themselves off from the main army. Appian tells us that Crixus, one of the slave-leaders, was at the Garganus Mountains, on the east coast of Italy, with thirty thousand men, and that after the defeat and slaughter of two-thirds of these troops by Gellius Publicola, Spartacus decided to head north. This separation has been interpreted as the result of arguments within the slave army, but there is very little to go on. Plutarch does say they had separated because of their insolent arrogance, but this does not necessarily mean that there had been a split. Whether Spartacus and the main army were ever at the Garganus Mountains is unclear, as too is their aim in going there at all.

The sources generally represent the ex-slaves as not recognising that their best hope of success and survival lay in complete obedience to Spartacus. Sallust, for instance, gives some lurid details although it is not clear when the events he is describing took place:

> Contrary to the orders of their general, the fugitive slaves immediately began to rape young girls and married women ... [killing] those who tried to resist them and who were trying to escape, inflicting wounds on them in a depraved manner, when their backs were turned, and left in their trail the torn bodies of half-dead persons .... Nothing was too sacred or too wicked to be spared the rage of these barbarians and their servile characters. Spartacus himself was powerless to stop them, even though he repeatedly entreated them to stop.

In any case, the Romans for once were successful. They destroyed this army of Germans, including Crixus.

In the meantime the other consul, Cornelius Lentulus, and his legion surrounded Spartacus and his army on their way north. Again we have only a notice of the result of this fighting without any specific location. Spartacus' troops defeated the Romans and also seized their supplies. This long journey from south of Rome to the Alps is passed over very swiftly by all the sources, but it is important to remember how far they went. They crossed the Apennines and reached the Alps with one consular army ahead of them and one behind.

The Romans themselves facilitated this travel, since they prided themselves on their roads. Their communications system was now used by their enemies to good effect. The startling distance covered by the insurgents is impressive in itself. As we saw earlier, Mithridates, according to Appian, observed that the

Italians allowed the Spartacan army through their land because they resented the Romans. Sallust also comments that slaves were sympathetic allies and uncovered things their masters had hidden away, or dragged out their masters themselves from their hiding places. This refers only to an incident in an unspecified town but presumably was true elsewhere too.

In engagements which again are not narrated in detail by our sources, Spartacus and his men defeated both consular armies. Paradoxically the Roman armies, by attacking the rebels, helped to maintain them. In every case, once victorious, the slaves were able to make use of the well-supplied Roman forces. After demolishing the attempts of the two praetors to subdue the insurgency, the rebels without apparent difficulty vanquished two legions led by consuls. The situation could not have been worse for the Romans.

However, according to Plutarch there were troops waiting to meet the ex-slaves in the north. The Roman governor of the province of Cisalpine Gaul, Gaius Cassius Longinus, went out to meet approaching rebel troops with what we are told was 'many thousands of soldiers'. Once again Spartacus and his army are victorious in a battle, this time near Mutina, but again there are no further details except that Cassius himself was nearly killed but escaped with difficulty (although one source, Orosius, says he was killed).

So far, then, with the exception of the Germans under Crixus, the slave army was undefeated. They had left Capua and headed southwards, moved across the peninsula to the east coast, then turned north all the way to the Alps, a journey of more than three hundred miles, overcoming all the forces the Roman Empire could send out against them. If they were intending to leave Italy, then there was nothing to stop them. However, mysteriously, having purposefully and successfully marched their way through the Italy and reached the Alps, overcoming all opposing armies, they turned and headed southwards again. Why head to the Alps in the first place?

Plutarch thought that the initial plan had been to leave Italy. The main elements in the group of seventy or so gladiators who had formed the original band were Gauls and Thracians, and Plutarch says that Spartacus' plan was for the army to disperse to their homelands, some to Thrace and others to Gaul, but that his followers had other ideas and preferred to pillage Italy. Of course by this time it cannot have been the case that most of the army were either Gauls or Thracians. Crixus, we are told by Plutarch, commanded the thirty thousand Germans. Sallust said Crixus' followers were Gauls and Germans. So it may be that the bulk of Spartacus' current forces had no interest in leaving Italy, or at least not via the Alps. Whatever the case, the army did change direction eventually and head south. There does seem to have been some change of mind, although of course we are not privy to this, or it could be that they were not heading towards the Alps in order to leave Italy. It was a long journey to take only to change one's mind.

The march on Rome

The sources interpret the decision to turn round as arrogance on the part of the ordinary slaves, who had become drunk with success and conceived the idea of marching on Rome itself. However only Florus and Appian record this plan, which, like the march across the Alps, was abandoned. Appian gives a rather colourful picture, reporting that Spartacus offered three hundred Roman soldiers as a human sacrifice for his general Crixus and then with his hundred and twenty thousand men marched towards Rome, torching all supplies, killing all prisoners and slaughtering all pack animals to speed his journey. Appian, though, gives us a rather negative representation generally. Although there was little to demoralise the slave army or let them think an attack on Rome would fail, they abandoned the idea and turned round yet again. Rome was on the brink of the utmost barbarian attack and was saved by the lack of courage of a slave, according to this scenario. The fear of an attack on Rome is recorded by Plutarch after the introduction of Crassus into the story. Here it is discord within the rebel army that puts paid to that idea.

There is clearly a lot missing from the ancient sources, which in any case are very brief. In a couple of sentences, if they mention this at all, Spartacus moved from the Alps to the southernmost part of Italy, a journey of well over seven hundred miles, having had the intention of leaving Italy, attacking Rome and then taking southern cities. It is impossible to tell what his intentions were. But the fact remains that he and his men undertook the enormous journey of travelling the length of Italy and back, over the course of months. It would have been far easier for them, after leaving Capua, to head immediately for Brundisium, as we are told they did eventually, and take to ships, if they had really wanted to leave Italy in the first place.

The mystery of their journey up and down Italy is one that makes no sense, unless they were not trying to leave. If they really had such internal arguments that they could not decide on where they were heading, then it is scarcely credible that they could have been so successful in repelling any Roman army that came close. It is widely accepted today, as we saw in the previous chapter, that the slave army had no large aims. Maria Wyke, for instance, writes:

> Several more recent analyses of the ancient evidence have concluded that Spartacus was not a revolutionary, that he did not proffer systematic opposition to the power and the rule of Rome nor plan to remodel Roman society, but probably had as his limited design the restoration of the largely foreign slaves to their respective homelands.[1]

The intentions of ancient characters are of course immensely interesting, but must always remain in the realm of speculation, especially when we consider how difficult it is to fathom those of people still alive and available for questioning today. It is rather more fruitful to examine achievements and from them perhaps extract possible intentions. If Spartacus had always intended to leave Italy, he showed profound ignorance of the geography of that peninsula, for it would have been far simpler and faster to travel east-west than north-south. What we can say safely is that the slave army was very successful militarily for a very long time.

Appian, who generally, as noted before, is rather more negative than Plutarch towards Spartacus, gives us two interesting pieces of information about the slave army. The first, as we have seen, is that Spartacus divided the profits from raiding equally and this attracted more followers to his camp. This policy helps to explain why Spartacus was so popular. One might add that he had some idea of equality, which clearly would be popular with slaves. Perhaps Appian tells us this in order to try to account for the horrible success of this enemy of Rome.

The second piece of information is that Spartacus did not allow merchants to bring in gold or silver and he did not allow his own men to acquire any. So there was no trade in these valuable metals. However he did buy iron and copper and allowed others to do so too. 'For this reason, the slaves had large quantities of basic materials and were well supplied and able to stage frequent raids.' And Appian adds that they always raided Roman supplies after a victory. There is a hint here of the moral superiority of the slaves, as if gold and silver corrupted men (which was a popular moralising theme in the late Republic and afterwards). In fact Pliny the Elder specifically makes this point in his *Natural History* when discussing these precious metals. In a comparison that Plutarch would have liked, he says:

> But we know that Spartacus forbad anyone in his camp to possess gold or silver, so much stronger at that time was the moral fibre of our runaway slaves. The orator Messala has recorded that the triumvir Antony used gold chamber-pots for

all the calls of nature, a charge that would have shamed even Cleopatra.

It is perhaps a little surprising that we do not get the detail about forbidding precious metals in Plutarch's account. He had been careful to inform his readers that Crassus had vast numbers of slaves and that he had silver mines, and this comparison of the extravagant wealth of the Roman with the austerity of the slaves would have helped his moral case, as we shall see in a later chapter.

4

Crassus

Spartacus now posed an enormous and increasing threat to Roman stability. He and his men had defeated the armies of two praetors, two consuls and the governor of Cisalpine Gaul with apparent ease. The ex-slaves were still at large, roaming the Italian countryside, spreading revolt among slaves from the Alps to the south of the peninsula. Their numbers were increasing as they travelled, and they had to be stopped. It is impossible to get a true idea of how many were in the rebel army from the sources. However, several sources suggest a figure in the region of a hundred thousand.

Appian tells us that by the time the Roman noble, Marcus Licinius Crassus, was asked to take over the command, which he did late in the year 72 BC, the war was then in its third year. The rebellious slaves had been fighting and moving up and down the Italian peninsula for over two years. The situation was desperate. Why Crassus? Why was he more likely to succeed than two consuls?

The situation in Rome at this time was hardly normal. Gaius Marius had marched on Rome in 87 BC, at which point Crassus had gone into hiding. He supported Sulla in the civil war a few years later and emerged as a powerful figure along with Pompey. Crassus had been a praetor in 73 BC and the normal career path would have been for him to go out to a province. However he had not done this, preferring to stay in Rome to prepare for the most coveted office of all, the consulship. Generals in Rome now had power independent of the offices they held, often because they could pay armies themselves, and Crassus was extremely rich. He recruited six legions and took over the two consular legions already in the field. The stakes were much higher and the rebels were about to face a massive onslaught. Plutarch adds that many Roman nobles joined Crassus against the slaves, giving as an explanation his good reputation and his friendship, but one might also suggest that they were very keen to get rid of the slave threat.

The main reason we know as much as we do about Spartacus is that Plutarch wrote the life of Crassus, as having been an important and influential politician in Rome. Part of the reason that the evidence we have of the early activities of Spartacus is not very full, even though the events were so momentous, is that Plutarch was only building up the picture before introducing Crassus. Once Crassus appears, Plutarch is on to his main subject, for whom, however, he had little admiration:

> Certainly the Romans say that in the case of Crassus many virtues were obscured by one vice, namely avarice; and it did seem that he only had one vice, since it was such a predominant one that other evil propensities which he may have had were scarcely noticeable.

Crassus, as depicted by Plutarch, was excessively greedy and had acquired his great wealth by buying up burning houses in Rome and then repairing them. 'In this way most of Rome came into his possession', remarks Plutarch, but one must allow for some exaggeration here.

An illustration of his desire for lucre is the rumour of a liaison between Crassus and a Vestal Virgin. Vesta was the goddess of the hearth, which with its everlasting flame symbolised the family and the state. It was a grave matter if the fire went out. The Vestal Virgins had the responsibility of ensuring that it did not, and they could only do this if they were chaste. Oddly, their temple contained not only the symbolic fire but also an erect phallus. If the Vestal Virgins were thought not to have remained celibate they were buried alive, the theory being that if they were innocent the goddess Vesta would rescue them. None was rescued in this way. So for Crassus to be accused of any intrigue of this kind could have had serious consequences for the woman.

It turned out, however, that this rumour arose from the fact that Crassus was pursuing the Vestal Virgin because he wanted to purchase her house cheaply. Plutarch says that Crassus was acquitted of having corrupted her because the judges knew how greedy he was, and therefore they believed that he was not after her body, only her house. Plutarch ends the story by saying that Crassus did not stop pestering the priestess until she sold him her house. He also owned silver mines and estates and earned money from the vast quantity of the slaves he owned. He is supposed to have said that no one could be called rich who could not support an army out of his income.

4. Crassus

Further rebel victories

It was this wealthy noble who was called upon by the Senate to fight the slave war. He recruited six new legions, almost thirty thousand men, and took over the two consular legions, as mentioned before, thus ending up with an army of almost forty thousand. It seems that by this time the Spartacan army had marched past Rome and was heading south. Crassus stationed his troops either on the borders of Picenum, an area on the east coast mentioned by both Appian and Plutarch, or near Picentia, which was south of Rome and of the previous rebel hideout at Vesuvius. He sent his legate Mummius with two legions on a long diversion, telling him to approach the rebel army from the rear but also giving him strict instructions not to attempt anything. Mummius however used his initiative and, thinking that he had a good opportunity, rushed into battle and was defeated. Again this episode is not in Appian's account. Plutarch is unspecific about location or tactics, and all we know is that the Romans incurred heavy losses and – even worse – that many dishonourably dropped their weapons and fled. The Romans had again underestimated their foes to their loss. However Crassus did not make this mistake. And he wanted to ensure that his men did not disobey him or forget what they were sent to do in future. The method he used to instil this discipline was decimation.

Decimation was the worst punishment soldiers could receive. One man out of every ten was randomly selected to be clubbed to death by his colleagues. This was held in reserve for extreme behaviour such as disobedience or cowardice. There are different versions of this episode. Plutarch writes that Crassus chose five hundred of those who had run off first and decimated them, so by this account fifty men would have been executed. However, Appian tells us that there is a version that says that Crassus himself lost a battle with his entire troops against Spartacus and decimated his whole army, in which case about four thousand men would have been killed. Whatever the truth, Crassus' decimation was an important factor in the telling of this story. After this terrible punishment, the Roman army proved more successful and started to win some battles. Whether this is because they feared their own commander at least as much as the enemy is unknown, but this is the impression we are given by the sources.

The legate Mummius does not feature in Appian's account, which merely records Crassus' first engagement with Spartacus as being a failure and says that after this defeat, he decimated his army. Then Crassus noticed that ten thousand of Spartacus' followers had split off from the main body of the slave army, and he destroyed two-thirds of them (with details rather similar to those of the Crixus episode) and then marched against the rest, beat them and drove them to the sea where he built a wall round them. Crassus was proving a stronger opponent than the generals sent out earlier.

Plutarch, however, records that Spartacus and his men, after their victory over Mummius, crossed Lucania to the north of the instep of Italy and reached the sea at the Strait of Messina which divides Italy from Sicily. According to some accounts Spartacus wanted to sail to Sicily simply to get away. But another possible version, as we have seen, is that he wished to ship two thousand men over to incite rebellion there, since it had only recently, or relatively recently, been extinguished. In both scenarios one might think he was trying to take the island of Sicily, since if he went over with all his men, that was a huge army.

Just as the Italian countryside seems in some sense at least to have been favourable, or at least not as hostile as it might have been, to the roving slave army, so the Mediterranean was not completely controlled by the might of the Roman Empire. There were independent operators who seem to have played a substantial role in the slave trade – pirates. Cilicia in southern Anatolia, modern Turkey, was famous in ancient times for its pirates. Plutarch relates that Spartacus had an arrangement with some Cilician pirates that they would transport him and his army over to Sicily, but they, as befits criminals perhaps or slave-traders, did not keep their word. Another possibility is that Verres, the governor of Sicily later prosecuted by Cicero, had, as he claimed and as Cicero so caustically rejected, stopped the slaves landing on his island, perhaps not by force, but by 'persuading' the pirates not to convey their cargo. Florus says that the slaves in their desperation

> tried to cross the swift-moving waters of the strait between the mainland and the island by using rafts made of wooden beams and barrels lashed together with thin vine tendrils, but in vain.

And the fragments of Sallust's history seem to record the same idea. Whatever the truth, the rebel army proceeded to head for Rhegium, a little further south, still looking across to the island.

Crassus then had the idea of building a wall and trench across the toe of Italy, which seems an incredible idea to us, since the distance must have been some thirty-five miles, even though we do not know exactly where the wall was built. It was an enormous project and must have seemed terrifying to the slaves. They had tried and failed to get across the water to Sicily and now they saw this incredible building programme walling them into their cul de sac. However, one night Spartacus and his men filled in part of the trench (with corpses of cattle and prisoners, says one hostile source) and simply marched across. One modern scholar has found the enterprise too unlikely and has suggested that Spartacus was on the promontory of Scyllaeum (north of Rhegium, overlooking the channel separating Italy from Sicily) when he was trying to get across to Sicily and that Crassus built a trench that simply traversed this promontory, not the whole toe of Italy.[1] However Plutarch is quite specific in asserting that this was an immense building project. It was, he says, fifteen feet wide and deep and had a strong wall protecting it; it was also about thirty-five miles long (by comparison, Hadrian's Wall is eighty-four miles long) and, thought Crassus, building it had the benefit of keeping his soldiers busy.

Appian says that the slave army sustained large losses as they tried to cross the trench and that Crassus' men killed six thousand of them in the morning and six thousand in the evening with the loss of only three Romans killed and seven wounded.

The reason, says Appian, for the Romans' eagerness for victory was their recent punishment. Appian also writes that Spartacus crucified a Roman prisoner to remind his own men what would happen to them if they lost, clearly sharing Crassus' motivational tactics, at least in Appian's view.

Some of Spartacus' men split off and camped by themselves by a lake in Lucania. Again we do not know that there was any argument within the rebel army, merely that a group of men had camped away from the main body. In any case, Crassus attacked them but Spartacus and his troops came to the rescue and drove off the Romans. Again this conveys the message that the ex-slaves by themselves could not cope without Spartacus – they needed direction, a master even. In most of the historical accounts Spartacus is accorded a phenomenal ability, and the slaves are portrayed as mere rabble who ultimately bring their leader down. Appian even says

> no city had come over to his [Spartacus] side, but only slaves, deserters and the flotsam and jetsam of humanity.

This has been repeated as if it were a failing on the part of Spartacus and his men, but it would have been extremely odd if a city had decided to come over to the side of the slaves. Those in the cities would all have had slaves themselves, so had they joined Spartacus *en masse* in effect they would have been handing over their lives to their own slaves. Unless the slaves who lived there had taken over the cities themselves, there is no way that a city could have joined the rebel forces.

The sources do not agree with each other when describing what happened next. Plutarch says that Crassus himself had asked the Senate to recall Pompey and Lucullus so that they could come and help him against Spartacus; Appian simply says that the Senate thought the war had been going on long enough and summoned Pompey on their own initiative. In any case Crassus heard that Pompey, his rival from the past, was heading to Italy after successes in Spain against Sertorius who had also rebelled against Rome. The need to defeat Spartacus before Pompey stole his victory became pressing.

After it is reported that Pompey is on his way, Appian tells us that Spartacus offered to negotiate with Crassus. We are not told the terms, only that it was refused with scorn. Then Spartacus is said to have headed towards Brundisium but, learning that the great general Lucullus was disembarking there after his victory over Mithridates, fell into despair.[2] It was then, according to Appian, that he turned to face Crassus, presumably knowing that all was lost. The difference in the accounts of what happened next is striking.

The following story appears only in Plutarch's description but seems to be a version of a shorter episode in Appian's which occurred earlier. A group of slaves, led by men called Gannicus and Castus, had separated from Spartacus and were making their own army camps. Again there is no notion of a split, just that they were separate from the main army. Crassus had sent six thousand soldiers to climb up to a ridge overlooking this smaller camp but remain hidden, a difficult task for six thousand men. Indeed they were spotted by two women from the slave camp, in a peculiar little detail. These two women had left their fellows for their menstrual period and gone up the mountains. From there they saw the Roman soldiers. The slaves attacked and were winning until Crassus led a detachment to rescue his men. Plutarch describes this as 'the hardest of all battles he [Crassus] ever fought'. The Romans were said to have killed twelve thousand three hundred, only two of whom had wounds in their backs. The resistance of the slaves is described as remarkable; they were fighting to the end. There would be no surrender.

Spartacus and his men retreated to the mountains of Petelia on the toe of Italy, on the east coast facing the heel. They were pursued by Lucius Quintus, officer under Crassus, and the quaestor Gnaeus Tremelius Scrofa. Generally after Crassus' troops had become involved, it seems to have been the policy, attributed to Spartacus, to avoid open conflict, but for once the rebel army turned and fought, and this time the Romans fled. This victory was Spartacus' undoing, however. His men, we are told, encouraged by this victory, became too confident and refused to carry on retreating. However in this change of tactic they were playing into Roman hands. Crassus had hoped to provoke this battle because he was keen to finish the matter before reinforcements came and stole his victory.

When the army was being drawn up for battle, Spartacus' horse was brought to him but, says Plutarch, he

> drew his sword and shouted that if he won the battle, he
> would have many fine horses that belonged to the enemy but

if he lost he would have no need of a horse. With that, he killed the animal.

This seems slightly unusual to the modern reader, but presumably it is a sign that Spartacus knew that he was going to lose and that he would die with his men, on his own feet. There was a previous incident involving a horse, in which the Roman praetor Varinius' horse was captured, as if horses are symbols of leadership and show that one can master the natural world for one's own advantage. Spartacus, by giving up his own horse, even killing it, might seem to show that he rejects leadership if that means giving himself an advantage over his own men.

Plutarch's description of Alexander the Great and his horse Bucephalus is relevant here. Alexander was able to tame a creature much physically stronger than himself by his perception and intelligence – brain over brawn one might say. Similarly Alexander controlled a massive army and marched into India by the same use of his intelligence. His army could not have taken all these places by force; normally he took control by his ability to manipulate people, by making them love and respect, and therefore obey him. Spartacus, here, voluntarily accepts a handicap to lose himself in the thick of the fighting and show moral leadership for his men. He will not fight under easier conditions than they do. According to Plutarch, having made this gesture Spartacus then rushed towards Crassus, who presumably was on his horse, but although he killed two centurions on the way he never reached him. Spartacus fought on, even while others had fled, until he was killed.

Even Appian describes the final battle in heroic terms:

Since so many tens of thousands of desperate men were involved [the slaves were desperate because they knew they would be killed if they were defeated and the Roman soldiers because they knew they still had a one in ten chance of being killed if they survived a defeat], the result was a protracted battle of epic proportions.

Spartacus was wounded but carried on fighting until he was killed. There were so many rebels killed that it was not possible to count the bodies. The Romans on the other hand lost about a thousand men, which is was not bad going – fewer than if Crassus had decimated his army.

Appian, the source more favourable to Crassus, points out that he achieved this great success in a mere six months. Crassus was not completely successful in keeping Pompey out of the story, however. Five thousand survivors of Spartacus' army ran into Pompey's army and he slaughtered them, claiming that although Crassus had won the battle, he, Pompey, had extinguished the war to its very roots. In any event Pompey was not telling the truth since we are told that ten years later, in 61 BC, the father of the future emperor Augustus is said to have destroyed the remnants of the fugitive slaves who had once fought for Spartacus and for Catiline. These ex-slaves were occupying the countryside around Thurii, a city which Appian says Spartacus captured, further up the coast from Petelia. This was such an important operation that Augustus, we are told, was given the nickname Thurinus, meaning the man from Thurii, because of this action of his father's.

The aftermath

It is only in Appian's history that we learn that Crassus pursued the survivors, who were still a large force and split into four, into the mountains and killed all but six thousand of them. These he had crucified along the road from Capua to Rome, a distance of about a hundred and twenty-five miles, so that there would have been a dead slave every forty metres or so along the way. This crucifixion is what many people today think of when they hear the name Spartacus, thanks to the Kirk Douglas film, although in fact the sources all claim that Spartacus died fighting, not hanging on a cross to have a last word with his wife and son. However the scene along the Appian Way, so vividly described at the start of Howard Fast's novel, must have indeed been at least as dramatic as that portrayed on celluloid. Not only were there miles of crosses along this major highway, but for a while there must have been screams of agony until all the victims died. And after death it was usual to leave the bodies to rot, so the senses would also have been overwhelmed by the stench of decaying flesh.

Alexander the Great had two thousand survivors from the siege of Tyre crucified, so it was not a purely Roman phenomenon, although they did use it fairly frequently. It was the worst form of punishment as it was so painful and lingering. It usually took place in a public place as a deterrent. Since one of the main objects was deterrence the authorities were keen for the victims to stay alive as long as possible and the swiftness of the end depended upon how the victim was fastened to the cross.

One of the most important parts of the aftermath for the Romans was the recovery of five Roman eagles, twenty-six battle standards, booty and five bundles of rods and axes, the very symbols of Roman authority and superiority. Each century, cohort and legion had its own standard. Often these had animal insignia on them. The most important was the eagle, the symbol of a legion. These standards, long poles with signs at the top, performed an important practical function, giving the unit a visible focus in battle high up above the action so that the unit could remain together. But they were also of huge symbolic significance, and losing one's standard was a terrible disgrace. It would have been a relief for the Romans to recover them, but it remained a dishonour that they had lost them at all.

Why did Crassus succeed where others had failed?

Crassus had more troops than Spartacus' previous opponents. The plan to go to Sicily was thwarted. We do not know why the pirates changed their minds about transporting the slaves. Verres may indeed have played some part in protecting Sicily, since it was certainly in his interest to do so despite Cicero's apparent refutation of this. Sallust credits Verres with having protected Sicily at least. Then the combined forces of Pompey and Lucullus heading towards Italy forced the rebels into a confrontation they had been at pains to avoid. With enemies coming from all quarters and without the revolt of other slaves throughout Italy, they were defeated.

Crassus was awarded an *ovatio*, 'ovation', for this victory. An ovation was less than a triumph, and this was because the war had been against slaves, not 'proper' enemies. However he managed to get himself awarded a crown of laurel, which was customary for triumphs, whereas myrtle was normally given for ovations.

5

Slaves after Spartacus

We know of no slave rebellion after Spartacus' that was as successful as his had been and certainly none as famous. Slaves continued to rebel and gladiators especially were considered dangerous, but it seems that the Romans had learnt their lesson well. Slaves were said to have been involved less than a decade after Spartacus in the Catilinarian conspiracy in 63 BC when the aristocrat Catiline, having failed to be elected consul twice, enlisted supporters to stage an armed insurrection. Ten years later, Milo, another Roman politician, organised gangs of mercenaries and gladiators and led them against rival forces led by another noble, Clodius, in Rome. In the following decade of civil war featuring Julius Caesar and Pompey, again there was talk of the involvement of slaves. But all these disturbances were instigated and led by Romans. When, for instance, the Senate passed a bill limiting the number of gladiators anyone could keep in Rome, it was because they were frightened of Caesar, not of the rebellious instincts of the gladiators.

Historians are of course more than mere observers. They form our very notion of the past and influence not only what we consider the important events of that past but our very selection of the events that we consider 'history'. This has long been observed by women, since until very recently women have mostly simply not been included in historical accounts. Our knowledge of the Sicilian and Spartacan slave wars is very much the result of the attentions of Diodorus, Plutarch and Appian, without whom we would have only passing references – which is all we have, generally, about later rebellions.

For example, there is a brief notice in the work of a Greek historian called Cassius Dio about some Spanish slaves who in 19 BC killed their masters, returned home and persuaded many to join them, planning attacks on Roman garrisons. Agrippa, general of the emperor Augustus, eventually defeated them but not without many defeats first. In a couple of other cases gladiators are involved, such as in AD 21 when the Aedui tribe rebel – part of their army is reported to be slaves training to be gladiators. In AD 64 during the reign of Nero there was a breakout by gladiators at Praeneste, twenty-five miles south of Rome.

In Sicily, perhaps at the end of the first century BC, a hundred years after the second Sicilian war, we learn that there was a man called Selouros, also known as 'son of Etna' because he and his bandit gang controlled the area round Etna for a long time. We do not know that he was a runaway slave, but he caused the authorities problems until he was arrested and sent to Rome to fight in the gladiatorial games. In fact he was not given a chance to fight for his life. In what follows we see that the Romans had an imaginative sense of the spectacular: Selouros was placed on a high contraption which somehow resembled Etna, so clearly his reputation had gone before him. The contraption was built in such a way that it suddenly collapsed, casting Selouros down into cages of wild beasts that had been placed below and built to fall open easily.

In AD 24, during the reign of the emperor Tiberius, there was a plot of rural slaves led by a former member of the praetorian guard, which however never seems to have started properly. The historian Tacitus, who tells us about it, says it would have been the beginning of another slave war. However, the plot was discovered before anything happened, and the leader and his associates were taken to Rome. Tacitus comments:

> Rome was already in a state of terror because the great number of domestic slaves was increasing beyond counting, while the free population was declining all the time.

So the fear of a slave war remained with the Romans even though they did not have another. Perhaps it is because of this great fear that another slave war did not break out – that is, the Romans took precautions.

A similar case to that of Selouros is recorded by Cassius Dio. In the third century AD an Italian named Bulla collected a bandit gang of about six hundred and raided Italy for about two years. Armies were sent out against him but were unable to defeat him. No one knew anything about him although he himself gathered information to keep ahead of his enemy.

Bulla even pretended to be someone else and went to the authorities to lay charges against himself, promising to lead a centurion to the bandit leader, but instead trapping and capturing him. Instead of killing the centurion, Bulla dressed up as a Roman magistrate and ordered the centurion to go back and say 'Tell your slave masters that they should feed their slaves enough so that they do not turn to a life of banditry'. The text which reports this goes on to say that most of his men were slaves from the emperor's household, some of whom had received little pay and others no sustenance at all, which seems very strange.

The emperor Severus was very angry at his troops' inability to cope with Bulla. Once again betrayal was the only way he could be caught. Bulla had been sleeping with another man's wife and this woman and her husband gave him up to the authorities.

When Bulla was put on trial, the praetorian prefect asked him, 'Why did you become a bandit?' Bulla's famous reply was, 'Why did you become a praetorian prefect?' He was thrown to the wild beasts and his gang of men disintegrated without him.

Other forms of resistance

Although there was no all-out war after Spartacus, there were other ways slaves could resist their lot. What is sometimes called servile misbehaviour may in fact be resistance. And it is not true that slaves did not cause further problems, as we have already seen. As we hear from a writer called Aulus Gellius, in the reign of Caligula, a slave named Androcles was due to appear in the Circus Maximus in Rome to be torn part by wild beasts. The crowd was amazed and delighted when the lion refused to attack Androcles. They set both of them free and gave Androcles the lion as a pet.

Caligula asked him why the lion had not attacked him and Androcles told him that while he was running away from his master he had hidden in the lion's den and taken a splinter out of his paw. They had been friends since then. However Androcles was arrested, sent back to his owner and condemned to death for having tried to escape.

In the course of this tale these words are put into Androcles' mouth:

> 'When my owner was governor of Africa, I was driven to run away by the unjustified beatings I received from him every day. And to make my hiding places all the more safe from him, I took refuge in isolated plains and deserts, intending if I should not find food somehow to kill myself ....'

So Androcles' response to cruelty was to run away and if he could not survive, then to kill himself. But of course the owner would see it as disobedience, laziness, an inability to do his job properly.

Therefore when we read about the 'deviant behaviour' of slaves, we may in fact be reading about slave resistance. This could range from lying, cheating, stealing, pretending to be sick, working slowly, petty sabotage and running away, to more violent acts such as suicide or murder. It is clear from laws that Romans saw suicide attempts by slaves as common. When a slave was sold, an edict required the seller to say whether the slave had tried to kill himself, and the sale could be cancelled if a slave turned out to be suicidal. For the case of the gladiator who suffocated himself with a toilet sponge, see p. 31.

For those who turned their aggression outwards, there was a famous case from the reign of Nero when the city prefect, Pedanius Secundus, was murdered by one of his slaves. The two possible reasons given by Tacitus, the historian who tells us of this case, are worth noting: it was either because Pedanius, the master, had refused to free his slave after agreeing a price with him, or because they were both in love with the same boy. Roman law said that if a master was murdered – by anyone, not necessarily a slave – all the slaves in his household were to be executed. This was supposed to make the slaves keen to protect their master and is revealing of the way the Romans thought their slaves felt towards them.

Pedanius Secundus was very rich. There were four hundred slaves in his household, so a protest arose at the idea of killing so many. Tacitus purports to give us the speech made against this protest, arguing for the execution:

> 'Our ancestors distrusted their slaves. Yet slaves were then born on the same estates, in the same homes as their masters, who had treated them kindly from birth. But nowadays our huge households are international. They include every alien religion, or none at all. The only way to keep down this scum is by intimidation. Innocent people will die, you say. Yes, and when in a defeated army every tenth man is flogged to death, the brave have to draw lots with the others. Exemplary punishment always contains an element of injustice. But individual wrongs are outweighed by the advantage of the community.'

The protests did not save the slaves but may have saved the dead man's freedmen, that is freed slaves who were also in his household.

Another case, in which slaves murdered their master in his bath, provoked the following comment from Pliny the Younger:

So you see how exposed we are to all sorts of danger, insult and humiliation. And it is not the case that anyone can feel himself secure because he is indulgent and mild – masters are not killed with a just cause but as the result of sheer criminality.

Again we see the sentiment *quot servi tot hostes*, 'all slaves are enemies', and, as mentioned before, Synesius in the fourth century AD was still saying this:

Crixus and Spartacus, two infamous gladiators who had been intended to serve as expiatory sacrifices in the arena on behalf of the Roman people once escaped in Gaul. They armed themselves and in furtherance of a revolution started the most terrible slave war that the Romans had ever known. Praetors, consuls and the luck of Pompey were required to counter them and to save the country from the impending danger. The followers of Crixus and Spartacus were not from the same country as their leaders, nor were they of the same nation and only their common lot and their fate drew them together for the campaign. And this is only natural. For I believe every slave to be the enemy of his master when it appears possible to overpower him.

He makes this point in order to say that the Empire is in trouble from the Bagaudae, gangs of peasants causing problems in Spain and Gaul, which may be why he made the error that Spartacus escaped in Gaul. However, the main thing to note here is the sentiment that slaves are inherently hostile to their masters. It is not difficult to see why the ancients held this view in that they held it themselves in reverse, being inherently hostile to their slaves. The Spartans declared war every year on their helots in order to justify killing any of them at any time.

The ancients thought that some people were naturally slaves, but they could see that they were also human beings and that they might not like being slaves even though it was in their own best interests. The first exposition of this justification of slavery appears in Aristotle's *Politics*:

> Therefore all men who differ from one another by as much as the soul differs from the body or man from a wild beast (and that is the state of those who work by using their bodies, and for whom that is the best they can do) – these people are slaves by nature and it is better for them to be subject to this kind of control, as it is better for the other creatures I have mentioned. For a man who is able to belong to another person is by nature a slave ....

However we also know from Aristotle that not everyone shared this view since he also tells us in the same work:

> Then there are others who hold that controlling another human being is contrary to nature, since it is only by convention that one man can be a slave and another free; there is no natural difference, and therefore it cannot be just, since it is based on the use of force.

There are enough theories showing why slavery is a good and necessary thing to indicate that such opposition was well known. The Greeks understood that by describing ideal places they were also criticising existing societies. One such description can be found in Diodorus' *History*. He wrote about the Islands of the Sun on which there were no rich or poor, no slave or free, where the inhabitants did all the work and where there were no temples, no priests, no soldiers or crime and no guardians, as there had been in Plato's *Republic*.

It is sometimes argued that the Romans had a much more sympathetic view of slavery — that slaves were simply the product of misfortune which could happen to anyone. They seem to have differed from the Greeks in freeing many more slaves, or at least the evidence would appear to show that the slaves that the Romans freed became Roman citizens, whereas freed slaves in Athens did not become Athenian citizens. Many Roman citizens would therefore have been ex-slaves, which presumably had an effect on the Romans' views of slavery.

However there is a passage in Suetonius' life of the emperor Augustus which might appear to contradict such sympathy:

> He [Augustus] also thought it very important that the people should be kept pure and uncorrupted by any taint of foreign or slave blood; so he was very sparing in granting Roman citizenship, and set limits to the number of slaves that might be manumitted .... He was not satisfied with imposing all sorts of difficulties to prevent slaves from being given their freedom, and many more difficulties preventing them from being given full freedom .... He ruled in addition that no one who had

ever been chained or tortured should attain citizenship through any form of manumission.

There was a problem with the theory of natural slavery. If slaves were freed, as they apparently quite often were in the Roman world, how could they be natural slaves? The term for freeing slaves is manumission, which literally means 'sending by the hand'. In Athens, as we have seen, freed slaves were not granted citizenship as they were in Rome. Sometimes, though rarely, a slave might be made a citizen, but this was a separate act. The sort of case in which this happened was when freed slaves might be required to fight for the city. Manumission at Rome was either formal or informal. Formal meant that the slave was set free and given Roman citizenship. Informal meant that the slave had only a de facto freedom at the pleasure of the owner and no rights at all. Informal manumission was conferred by the master by letter or word of mouth in the presence of friends acting as witnesses.

There were of course several advantages for the master in freeing slaves. It meant he did not have to feed old or sick slaves, and that he could still receive money and services from slaves he had freed. Sulla is perhaps the best example of yet another advantage. Appian tells us that Sulla freed ten thousand slaves of proscribed persons, choosing the youngest and strongest, to whom he gave freedom and Roman citizenship. He called them Cornelii after himself. Appian explains dryly, 'In this way he made sure of having ten thousand men among the plebeians always ready to obey his commands.'

5. Slaves after Spartacus

The fact that Spartacus' revolt was the last substantial slave insurrection points to the enormous shock it gave to the Roman system. The Romans never again allowed themselves the carelessness that might risk such an uprising.

6

The Creation of a Hero

Without historians, history is simply an idea. Writers can form or deform our ideas of the past. They can also create heroes and villains. Without hagiographers the virtues of the saints would be interred with their bones. Usually individuals are famous because someone chose to record their deeds for posterity. Homer immortalised Achilles, Plato preserved the memory of Socrates, Medea's name would hardly be known had Euripides not written his play, St Antony's name would have perished without the pen of the bishop Athanasius. Julius Caesar took care of his own reputation.

Who enabled us to remember the name of Spartacus? How was it that a positive image of Spartacus was transmitted, even though the historians were all members of the slave-owning class, whose sympathies could never lie with rebellious slaves? As with many of our attitudes to the ancient world, the answer lies with Plutarch, one of the most influential writers from antiquity, but one who was writing over a hundred and fifty years after Spartacus.

Plutarch has been consistently popular, and thus influential, through the ages because he wrote such entertaining and unforgettable lives of Greek and Roman statesmen and generals. The *Parallel Lives* were translated into Latin, and then into Italian and Spanish in the fifteenth century and into German in the sixteenth. Jacques Amyot translated them into French and Thomas North translated Amyot's French into English in the sixteenth century. Shakespeare clearly recognised Plutarch's genius and not only used his work as a source of information but kept many of the anecdotes and best lines of the ancient writer.

Spartacus' historians

There are not many accounts of Spartacus. And very few from even the same century as the revolt. Sallust was a contemporary, but the work called the *Histories* in which he describes the events survives only in fragments. The broken sentences that we have are very confusing. Another contemporary, Cicero, makes passing mention in his speeches to the events of the late 70s, but there is no extended discussion. The references to Spartacus in the remaining works of the prolific and early writer Varro are unfortunately very few. In the same century, Livy wrote an enormously long history in 142 books of which only thirty-five survive in their original form. The references to Spartacus are from those that remain only in summaries and so are brief in the extreme. The same is true for the less ambitious Diodorus, the full length of whose universal history ran to only forty books.

Other writers who mention Spartacus are Velleius Paterculus and Frontinus writing in the first century AD, Florus in the second and Athenaeus a little later, but there is no detail. There is a page or so of the Christian historian Orosius from the fifth century AD, but generally Roman historians whose work survives do not explore what to modern readers is a revolutionary situation. Despite this dearth of information, however, Spartacus is not only well known, he is also popular.

The longest account apart from Plutarch's is by Appian, a Greek historian from Alexandria in Egypt who wrote a *Roman History* in the second century AD. Because he wrote a history and Plutarch wrote biographies, Appian is sometimes taken more seriously. Much of Plutarch's material has often been dismissed as gossip by modern historians, who have frequently failed to appreciate his masterpiece adequately. As we have already seen, the accounts of the two writers frequently diverge. If one were to prefer Appian's account, however, one would come away with the impression that Spartacus was too brutal an individual to be a popular hero.

It is sometimes claimed that it was a letter written by Karl Marx to Friedrich Engels saying he had been reading Appian that started the idolisation of Spartacus. As Zvi Yavetz writes:

> Once, returning wearily from his arduous work on *Das Kapital* at the British Museum, he read Appian in Greek for relaxation. In those moments he felt admiration for Spartacus and longed for a similar leader for the modern proletariat. In his enthusiasm he wrote to Engels on the subject in a letter which has been quoted religiously in every Marxist treatise since. Spartacus became the symbol of the revolution and an entire myth sprung up around him.[1]

From this passage it might be inferred that Marx's enthusiasm was responsible for the whole myth of Spartacus. His comments were very brief – what he actually said was:

> Spartacus emerges as one of the best characters in the whole of ancient history. A great general (unlike Garibaldi), a noble character, a genuine representative of the ancient proletariat. Pompey was a real shit.[2]

However it is unlikely that Marx reached this judgement without having read Plutarch. From Appian we learn that Spartacus sacrificed three hundred prisoners on the death of one of his generals, crucified a Roman soldier in front of his camp, and slaughtered prisoners and pack animals alike when it suited him. On the other hand Crassus, in Appian's narrative, won a brilliant victory and was distinguished by birth and wealth. To account for Spartacus' popularity, Appian says that he distributed equally any booty won from victories or raids. There are not many other positive qualities described in Appian's account, other than that merchants were not allowed to import gold or silver and that the men in Spartacus' army were not permitted to acquire any. Some have seen this as a sign of Socialism.

Appian says that Spartacus died fighting although his body was never found, and that the slaves were killed in the final battle, all but six thousand who were crucified along the road from Capua to Rome, as everyone knows who has seen the film. As seen earlier, in another work on the Mithridatic war, Appian says that almost all of Italy had revolted from the Romans because they hated them so much and had even sided with the gladiator Spartacus against the Romans, even though he was a wholly disreputable person.

So to get a positive picture of Spartacus you have to read the text of Appian very carefully and selectively and already be predisposed to like him. And yet what other kind of description could one expect? Slaves did not write their own history; we only know about them from the elite who won, who wrote the history and stamped their interpretation on events. It seems a remarkably independent mind that could idealise Spartacus from Appian's picture.

Plutarch and the Romans

It is in Plutarch's *Life of Crassus* that we read about Spartacus the hero. Plutarch does not tell us that Spartacus sacrificed three hundred Roman soldiers nor that he crucified another as a warning to his own men or to the Romans. Nor in fact does he give us the gruesome fact, found only in Appian, that six thousand ex-slaves were crucified along the Appian way. Plutarch tells us that Spartacus was big and strong and brave, intelligent and noble, and that, as mentioned before, when he was in Rome waiting to be sold as a gladiator a snake coiled up round his face signifying a great power that would bring him either misfortune or good fortune. Plutarch also tells us that the original band of gladiators shed their gladiatorial weapons as soon as they could because they were dishonourable and barbaric. This is unexpected coming from a band of Thracians and Gauls.

Plutarch describes how Spartacus tried to lead his men to their homelands but they had grander ideas and disobeyed him, looting and pillaging. His generalship won nine victories over the Romans, who eventually sent out Crassus. When Spartacus realised all was lost he killed his horse, threw himself towards Crassus, killing two centurions on the way, but not reaching the general. In the end, when all his men had abandoned him, he stood his ground alone, surrounded by the enemy, and was killed fighting to the last.

So Plutarch selects different events to describe from those Appian chose, ones that reflect better on the slave-leader. But what really proves Plutarch's sympathy beyond a shadow of a flicker of a doubt is the way he introduces Spartacus into his life of Crassus. He says that Spartacus was from Thrace and was strong and nobler and more intelligent that you would expect from a slave. He also says 'he was more Greek than his background would indicate'. From Plutarch this is praise indeed. Spartacus was not Greek, he was Thracian, as Plutarch had just pointed out, so why did Plutarch say this? In order to make his Greek-speaking readers like Spartacus. But why should they like him if he was not properly Greek? Perhaps more to the point, why did Plutarch paint such a positive picture of him? The conventional view of Plutarch is that:

> He was in his writing an active exponent of the concept of a partnership between Greece, the educator, and Rome, the great power, and of the compatibility of the two loyalties.[3]

This compatibility of the two loyalties is important because Plutarch wrote *Parallel Lives* of Greeks and Romans. He wrote

lives of pairs of individuals, in the vast majority of cases one
Greek and the other Roman. He not only wrote each life with
its pair in mind, but often added a formal comparison at the
end. It is normally stated that he is fair-minded and has no pref-
erence of Greek over Roman or vice versa, but saw the vices and
virtues of each individual.

Plutarch was a Greek living at a time when Greece was part of
the Roman Empire and there were Greek slaves in Rome, and
one might assume that he naturally preferred Greeks to Romans,
since comparisons call for such a judgement. If one reads only
Plutarch, and no works by modern scholars discussing Plutarch,
it is quite difficult to see the almost unnatural objectivity some
have observed. In very many cases in the *Parallel Lives*, the
Romans may be good generals but the Greeks are also good men.
Perhaps the best known example is the pair of lives of Alexander
the Great and Julius Caesar, where in almost every respect
Alexander emerges superior. Virtually the only good men the
Romans have among them are those who take Greek culture seriously, and even then they often cannot quite grasp the essentials.

Plutarch was rather more subtle than the above might imply,
but some lives stand out as having been written with undeniable
antagonism to certain aspects of Roman rule. About the great
general Marius he writes:

> It is said that Marius never studied Greek literature and never
> used the Greek language on any occasion that mattered. It was
> ridiculous, he thought, to study a literature which had to be
> taught by a subject race.

Plutarch was writing in Greek so presumably most of his readers were Greek. Even if they were Romans they would be included among those sophisticated citizens who made an effort, like Cicero, and so could feel that they were a cut above the average Roman. Another example is Sulla, who made the streets of Athens, the very centre of learning, culture and humanity, run with blood. Plutarch portrays him as an ugly bisexual buffoon and describes Sulla's horrific death of having his intestines turn into worms in unnecessary detail.

Plutarch's avowed aim in his *Parallel Lives* is to hold up examples of heroes for his readers to follow. However the *Life of Crassus* does not fit this aim as he hardly qualifies as a hero the way Plutarch describes him. Crassus is portrayed very negatively. He was excessively greedy, and we learn this in the first paragraph of his life. He acquired his wealth by buying up burning houses in Rome and then repairing them. He owned silver mines and estates and also earned money from the vast quantity of the slaves he possessed.

His Greek counterpart, the person with whom he is compared in the *Parallel Lives*, is Nicias, who was an Athenian general during the Peloponnesian War. Since he contributed to the disastrous failure of the Sicilian Expedition by his inaction at crucial moments, he is also perhaps a less than sympathetic character. However, in Plutarch's portrayal Nicias' main fault is that he is too pious. Crassus, on the other hand, the other half of this comparison, is insatiably greedy. For someone comparing the two, the vices are hardly equivalent.

Indeed there is an implicit contrast in the first paragraph of

Crassus' life where we learn that he was suspected of a liaison with a Vestal Virgin, although he really wanted to buy her house, as we have seen. Nicias is excessively pious and pays too much attention to omens and oracles. Crassus is so impious through his greed that he harasses a Vestal Virgin.

Also early on, in establishing Crassus' character, Plutarch stresses the vast numbers of slaves he possessed and used as a source of revenue. This stress on the huge numbers of slaves is surely deliberate on Plutarch's part, drawing attention to the poetic justice that Crassus would later find himself fighting slaves and risking being defeated by them.

Spartacus, one of that class of men exploited by Crassus in his own household, is held up by contrast. His character is noble. He cares about his men, about honour, about equality. Crassus emerges as the more barbaric character (notice that, as befits such a barbarian, he hates Cicero, who is one of the Romans most favourably portrayed in the *Parallel Lives*). Plutarch, by elevating Spartacus in this way, is continuing the negative portrayal of Crassus. Even a slave has more nobility of character than this Roman. There is no such episode in the *Life of Nicias*.

Plutarch was using the opportunity of the Spartacus episode to throw light on the character of Crassus. Plutarch liked comparisons and throughout the *Parallel Lives* he not only compares the two subjects of his pair but also makes internal comparisons in the individual lives. For example, in the *Life of Antony*, Cleopatra, another famous Roman hate-figure, was given extended treatment to highlight Antony's faults. Antony was stupid and driven by his passions. Plutarch says damningly:

> His character was, in fact, essentially simple and he was slow to perceive the truth.

Cleopatra, despite being a woman, is portrayed as having more ability in every sense than Antony. Of course she was also Macedonian, but by Plutarch's time this is hardly relevant. After all he was quite happy for Alexander the Great, also Macedonian, to be his Greek counterpart for Julius Caesar. Perhaps because she is a woman, Cleopatra's intelligence is portrayed as an ability to manipulate others. But intelligence was very important for Plutarch and always preferable to stupidity. Of Cleopatra, Plutarch says

> Plato speaks of four kinds of flattery but Cleopatra knew a thousand.

Mark Antony was putty in her hands. He showered gifts upon her which were no mere trinkets, Plutarch comments sarcastically – gifts like Phoenicia, Cyprus, a large part of Cilicia, part of Syria and Judaea and the coast of Arabia Nabataea.

Spartacus, then, had the nobility of character that one would expect from a Roman of Crassus' rank but which Crassus so signally lacked. Just as Cleopatra is built up to show just how stupid Antony was, so Spartacus is described at some length in order to show what a despicable character Crassus was. This theory does not entail too much imagination if one looks at Plutarch's words about Spartacus:

> He not only possessed great spirit and bodily strength [Greek: *rhomen*], but he was more intelligent and nobler than his fate, and he was more Greek than his [Thracian] background might indicate. People tell the following story about him when he was brought to Rome [Greek: *eis Rhomen*] to be sold as a slave .... ⁴

The word for strength is '*rhome*' which is the also the word in Greek for the city of Rome. The words '*rhomen*' and '*Rhomen*' are identical in form and very close to one another in the passage quoted above. They refer to totally different things, but they look exactly the same. In Greek one can see the similarity straightaway. We know that Plutarch was conscious of the possible pun or etymology for the word because in the opening words of his *Life of Romulus* he relates that some say that the Pelasgians named the city Rome (*Rhome*) because of their strength (*rhome*) in arms.

One thus could say that Spartacus embodied the very essence (*rhome*) of Rome, although he was only a gladiator. He possessed strength and many other laudable qualities; Crassus on the other hand was despicable in his lust for money and small-minded rivalry with Pompey. Spartacus thought only of his men and even when they did not listen to him, he did not abandon them but did his best. He died on his feet fighting, surrounded by enemies. Crassus' death was less dignified. First he was a useless general; while in Syria he neglected his army and devoted his time to making money. After a disastrous battle against the Parthians he lay in bed depressed, although his men needed his encouragement. He was murdered miserably while trying to make peace, and the final insult was that his severed head was used as a theatrical prop in a production of the play *The Bacchae*. There is little doubt where Plutarch's sympathies lie.

One could argue that Spartacus appears in a good light only because Plutarch was trying to denigrate Crassus, whom he clearly disliked. Nevertheless this dislike allowed a positive portrayal of a rebellious gladiator who otherwise would have been ignored or cast as a villain. This favourable verdict for a rebel is extraordinarily rare, although perhaps less rare in Plutarch, who was unashamedly on the side of those who rebelled against Rome. He also described a woman, Cleopatra, more extensively than ancient writers normally did. Cleopatra is a rather similar figure to Spartacus, in that she is loved by the general public but rather despised by the academic world.

Plutarch thus allows us a glance from a different angle, for he had his own agenda and he let slip details which slave-owners usually hide. Because he wanted to highlight the faults of a Roman, he allowed a contrast to emerge in his picture. In order to understand why he gave us this relatively detailed portrait of a slave we must see what else he was trying to show us. But for generations his story of Spartacus has attracted more attention than his main purpose, which was to show us the character of Crassus.

This is because this contrast is so unusual. Normally we read about the savage nature of slaves – and by the time the Christian historian Orosius in the fifth century AD writes about the episode the number of slaves has mushroomed to a hundred thousand and they are committing arson, theft, rape and murder. Orosius also narrates the lurid and most improbable story of a woman whom the slaves had raped and who as a consequence had killed herself. For some unexplained reason, however, the slaves give her an elaborate funeral and stage gladiatorial games using four hundred prisoners they have taken. This description is what we would expect to read of rebelling slaves, that they were barbarians who raped and drove to suicide and killed for fun. We do not expect to read about them that they were intelligent and noble individuals with a touch of the Greek about them.

But how do modern historians find the truth? What is the truth? Do the events of 73 to 70 BC merit more than a passing mention? The Easter Rising in Dublin in 1916 lasted less than a week, starting on Monday 24 April and ending on the Saturday. It is celebrated as one of the great events of Irish history. Spartacus' rebellion lasted for almost three years. But in the Irish case, there were many ready to take up their pens and write histories, songs and poems celebrating their action, and there were millions of Irish all over the world eager to read and hear about these events. People from the slave-owning class did write about Spartacus' actions, but they were generally hostile. However, a glimpse of a favourable picture slipped through via the biographical writings of a Greek, who had more than a sneaking admiration for those who rebelled against the mighty

Romans. For those who wish to see change, to see oppressed people rise up and fight back, Spartacus represents a great hero. Generally classicists in the West have not shared such aspirations. For them he is a footnote in the history of the late Republic whose real significance lay in the fact that his revolt was the catalyst for the estrangement of Crassus from Pompey.

Spartacus represented the worst threat the Romans could face. He was the enemy within. For a while he was better than the Romans at what the Romans did best. He beat them in battle not once but nine times. With every victory more slaves joined him, buoyed up by his success. He had to be beaten. The crucifixions along the road from Capua to Rome demonstrated publicly the Roman ferocity when they finally subdued him. He lost the final battle and his life, but he had fought harder and longer than any would have expected. One could perhaps argue that, from a very long perspective, he won the war.

Spartacus in the Modern Imagination

Kirk Douglas, in his autobiography *The Ragman's Son*, explains why he found the story of Spartacus so exciting:

> Spartacus was a real man, but if you look him up in the history books, you find only a short paragraph about him. Rome was ashamed; this man had almost destroyed them. They wanted to bury him. I was intrigued with the story of Spartacus the slave, dreaming the death of slavery, driving into the armor of Rome the wedge that would eventually destroy her.
>
> I'm always astounded by the impact, the extent of the Roman Empire. Caesarea, Israel – full of Roman ruins. In Tunisia, a coliseum. Roman ruins in England. How did the Romans get to so many places? Aqueducts everywhere. Travel is difficult now, by jet. But on horseback, or on foot? It always amazed me how they did that and how much they did.
>
> Looking at these ruins, and at the Sphinx and the pyramids in Egypt, at the palaces in India, I wince. I see thousands and thousands of slaves carrying rocks, beaten, starved, crushed, dying. I identify with them. As it says in the Torah: 'Slaves were we unto Egypt.' I come from a race of slaves. That would have been *my* family, *me*.

Douglas was clearly inspired by this heroic individual who, with no resources, had dared to fight against an Empire that controlled them all and stretched across the known world. He identified immediately with the slaves who had built the great monuments of civilisation and culture. Part of this point of contact was from his own Jewish background. His original name was Issur Danielovitch Demsky, and he was the son of a Jewish Russian immigrant, born in New York in 1916.

But even more important than his sympathy with this ancient figure, is how Douglas had come across him at all. He had read the novel *Spartacus* by Howard Fast. As argued in the previous chapter, the heroic stature this ex-gladiator has enjoyed was due initially to Plutarch, who has had immeasurable sway over modern sensibilities. In the twentieth century, however, the individual most responsible for the cultivation of the glamorous status of Spartacus was the American novelist, Howard Fast. It was indeed in novels in the twentieth century that conflicting views of Spartacus and his rebellion were played out. In academia, by contrast, the battle for the myth of Spartacus was really fought on only one side, since the response of Western academics was generally to ignore this historical figure.[1]

Spartacus as Christ-figure

There had in fact already been two novels written in English about Spartacus before Fast's. The first was by the Scottish author, Lewis Grassic Gibbon, whose real name was James Leslie

Mitchell. He was born in 1901 in Aberdeenshire and is famous for his *A Scots Quair* trilogy. Grassic Gibbon published *Spartacus* in 1933, three years before his early death at the age of thirty-five. He, like Fast, chose the subject from political commitment rather than antiquarian interest.

For Grassic Gibbon, Spartacus is the personification of the will of the people. He *is* the people and senses what they want, which is how Gibbon explains what looks like senseless wandering up and down the peninsula of Italy – the people change their minds. There is also an equation with Christ, since one could argue that Christ is the embodiment of human hope. The book starts and ends with the words

It was springtime in Italy, a hundred years before the crucifixion of Christ ....

Spartacus is tall and quiet. His generals argue among themselves and thus bring ruin to the slave army, but he does not complain. He does his best. He inspires love among his men, and sometimes this gives rise to rivalry among them. Fittingly perhaps for such a universally loved character, he is bisexual.

The reader sees the action through the eyes of an Athenian eunuch, Kleon, who is devoted to Plato's *Republic* and carries a copy of it round with him, trying to persuade Spartacus to follow its recommendations. Perhaps he represents true detached reason or mutilated pure reason. He is learned, described as a *literatus*, and is not sidetracked by women or boys. He knows that he is missing something and despairs at times, but Spartacus gives meaning to his life. The book ends with Kleon hanging on a cross shouting for Spartacus.

And he saw before him, gigantic, filling the sky, a great Cross with a figure crowned in thorns; and behind it, sky-towering as well, gladius in hand, his hand on the edge of the morning behind that Cross, the figure of the Gladiator. And he saw that these Two were One and the world yet theirs: and he went into unending night and left them that shining earth.

Failure of ideals

The second novel, *The Gladiators* by Arthur Koestler, was published in 1939. It paints a quite different picture. To counteract the popularity of Fast's book, Koestler's was reprinted in 1956. As Kirk Douglas was trying to get his film made, there was also a proposal to do a movie version of the Koestler novel starring Yul Brynner, but this came to nothing.

Koestler, who was born in Budapest in 1905, had been an active member of the Communist Party and had fought in the Spanish Civil War, being captured by Franco's troops at one point. He was disillusioned and embittered by the show trials in the late 1930s and left the party. His novel, written at this time as his comrades were being executed, is about how revolutions turn bad.

Koestler was interested in the resentment felt by the Italians and the rest of the Empire towards Rome. He describes this resentment very effectively, as well as the feelings of anger at injustice, but in his novel Spartacus is portrayed as being forced by circumstances to sell out. We see the inevitable failure of his ideals, and the constant internal arguments within the slave army.

Man's inability to unite is divinely ordained and inevitable, at least as shown here. An old man tells the story of the tower of Babel in which men build a huge edifice and God becomes jealous at their presumption so he makes them unable to understand each other and the enterprise fails.

There is an episode in which a slave returns to his master when the slave army begins to lose and his master, who had been a humane owner in the past, has sex with his slave saying

> 'You see this is also a solution and a way to enjoy one another. You can regard it as a symbol if you wish. For considering what the two of us are and represent I cannot think of anything better for us to do.'

Spartacus fails because the other slaves of Italy do not rise up. Rejection of slavery in one city will not work. All the slaves everywhere must rebel. The equation with Socialism in only one country being doomed to failure is more than clear. Koestler also ends a chapter saying that revolutions would not succeed

> until knowledge was no longer foisted on it [the people] from outside, but was born in laboured torment out of its own body, thus gaining from within power over the happening.

And he describes the slaves mindlessly following leaders without thinking for themselves.

More chilling is the repetition of the danger of men with good intentions. A rhetorician called Zosimus is given this cynical speech

'It is dangerous to combine so much power in the fist, and so many lofty reasons in the head of one single person. In the beginning the head will always order the fist to strike from lofty reasons; later on the fist strikes of its own accord and the head supplies the lofty reasons afterwards; and the person does not even notice the difference. That's human nature, my lad. Many a man has started out as a friend of the people and ended up as a tyrant; but history gives not a single example of a man starting out as a tyrant and ending up as a friend of the people. Therefore I tell you again: there is nothing so dangerous as a dictator who means well.'

Koestler used his novel as a warning against people with ideals who set out to make a better world. His view seems to have been that human nature is so bad that nothing good can ever come of this. Koestler is famous for his views on euthanasia and his own suicide. Perhaps understandably he is much hated on the Left, but this novel is not simplistic anti-Communism. It is a sad reflection on the failure of revolution. Koestler's sympathies clearly lay with the oppressed, but he could see no hope for them. The novel was first published in 1939 before his involvement with the CIA, when he took a more active role in denigrating the Left.

Spartacus as revolutionary hero

Howard Fast's approach to his subject was also directly political. He had planned his novel about Spartacus while in prison in 1950. A famous novelist, he had been jailed for refusing to supply a list of names of supporters of the Joint Antifascist Refugee Committee to the House Committee on Un-American Activities. The Joint Antifascist Refugee Committee had organised support and refuge for Spanish Republicans after Franco seized power in Spain. This was the McCarthyite period in America, when the Left was systematically being crushed after the great union upsurge in the 1930s and the wave of pro-Russian sentiment after the Second World War. As Fast describes vividly in his autobiography, *Being Red*, the Communist Party was once quite popular in the USA, though today this seems scarcely credible to those who did not witness the phenomenon.

While in prison Fast had grown depressed about the Communist Party, of which he was a member but which had tried to influence what he should or should not write. He was encouraged by the writings of Rosa Luxemburg, who had strong views on freedom, and he quoted some of her work in *Being Red*:

> Freedom for the supporters of the government only, for the members of one party only, no matter how big its membership may be is no freedom at all. Freedom is always freedom of the man who thinks differently. This contention does not spring from a fanatical love of abstract justice but from the fact that

everything which is enlightening, healthy and purifying in political freedom derives from its independent character and from the fact that freedom loses all its virtue when it becomes a privilege.

Fast records that his friend, Albert Malz, commented that there could have been no Soviet Union such as emerged after Stalin's rise to power if Luxemburg's ideas had won out. Fast started to think about why she and Karl Liebknecht had called their group the Spartakusbund. He read everything he could about the ancient slave revolt, even learning Latin as best he could, which was perhaps not the best approach as the main sources are in Greek. He had already written about slaves in the USA in his best-seller *Freedom Road*, so it was a not such an unnatural progression to write a novel about Roman slaves.

Fast's is no longer a household name, but in the late 1940s he was a best-selling author. He had been very surprised to be jailed and even more surprised when his new manuscript was enthusiastically received by his publisher but rejected for publication. It was turned down because J. Edgar Hoover, the head of the FBI, sent word that the book was not to be published. The editor resigned. Fast sent his novel to seven other publishers who all turned it down as a result of pressure from Hoover.

However one sympathetic bookseller, who was in charge of Doubleday bookshops, ordered six hundred copies of the book in advance. He advised Fast to publish it himself, telling him it was worth the financial risk. It certainly was. It sold several million copies and is still in print today.

In his novel, Fast gives quite a prominent place to a rebellious Jewish character called David, who is so numbed by the brutality and horror of slavery that he is emotionally dead until he meets Spartacus. David is crucified, and there is the most astonishingly graphic description of the unbearable pain of crucifixion and how it breaks up any rational thought. Fast describes his own experience of his appalling headaches in *Being Red*, so perhaps he put his personal experience into these descriptions. They are in any case very memorable. He makes a point of describing the popularity of crucifixions at that time, as if to comment that Christ's suffering was one of very many. At one point, in connection with religion, he states:

Spartacus hated the gods and gave them no worship.

Later, describing David dying on the cross, Fast writes:

In his suffering he did not call upon God, because in God there was no answer and no explanation. He did not believe any more in one God or in many gods. In that second time of his life, his relationship with God changed. God answered only the prayers of the rich.

As he is dying David shouts out 'Spartacus why did we fail?' and the reader then gets a flashback of his part in the rebellion. By the end he realises they had not failed, that by fighting back they had won. They had said yes to life, and for Fast Spartacus is not so much the will of the people as a love of life. Several times he says 'the secret of life is life', and Spartacus loves life however awful it is, insisting that his wife promise not to kill herself. She survives and is free at the end of the book.

Spartacus in Fast's novel is resolutely heterosexual and monogamous. Homosexuality is used to denote the decadence of the Romans, but he is politically correct on the subject of women, who fight and participate along with men. When describing Cicero, who has a largish minor part and who is thoroughly objectionable, Fast writes:

> Like so many young men of his type, he perpetually awaited the woman who would understand him – which meant the woman who would feed his ego properly.

His description of slavery draws considerably on US slavery, and the very direct details are graphically drawn. In Fast's novel, Spartacus has no rebellious, argumentative generals. He inspires love, unites people and leads and enthuses them and yet is constantly described as 'ordinary'. Fast describes how Spartacus was nearly killed and comments:

> But it is questionable whether it would have changed history too much if Spartacus had perished. The forces which prodded him would simply have turned elsewhere.

At the end of the novel Spartacus' wife describes him several times as pure, which drives Crassus wild. She explains that anyone would be pure who set their face against evil. It's a very simple fight in Fast.

The narrative is more complex than Gibbon's linear plan, consisting as it does of a series of flashbacks. Fast therefore does not concern himself too much with why the slaves go up and down Italy. Scenes switch between the slave army and the Romans. Fast devotes more space to the Romans, and his Roman characters are entertaining and by no means totally evil. Some have the right spirit if the wrong focus for their loyalty.

The battle for Spartacus

All three novels are still in print and they are still read today, not because they illustrate a proletarian world-movement or a first stage in Communism. What we get from them, and from the film, in spite of its shortcomings, is the underdog daring to fight back.

They all describe people with no resources fighting against those who hold all of them. Oppressed people who have nothing but numbers, brains and rage. The slaves are fighting for justice, for freedom and for a better society. They believe a better, different, world is possible, and this has resonance with many today.

Even in Koestler all these elements exist. For him the Romans are appalling exploiters, but he thinks nothing can be done about it. There are not even any sympathetic Romans such the figure of Gracchus in Fast's novel. Koestler's is a gripping but ultimately depressing novel. Fast's is an exhilarating and compulsive read and as a novel it has the power to keep its readers turning the pages, whatever their politics. And it was Fast's words that alerted Kirk Douglas to the potential of the story.

8

The 'Thinking Man's Epic'

Spartacus was a hero in the Communist bloc countries in the second half of the twentieth century. Primary schools, cinemas, football teams and children were named after him. Stalin put forward the theory, which was immensely influential, that the great slave uprisings of the declining Roman Republic annihilated the slave-owner class and the slave-owner society. But almost paradoxically, Spartacus' enduring fame today is due much more to a film made in Hollywood. Although there is no evidence that Kirk Douglas was remotely influenced by any events or ideology emanating from the East, his film was always political.

Immediately it was released there was a call for a boycott by the Legion of Decency, a Catholic organisation which was immensely powerful in the US at that time. The right-wing columnist Hedda Hopper advised, almost hysterically,

> It has acres of dead people, more blood and gore than you ever saw in your whole life. In the final scene, Spartacus' mistress, carrying her illegitimate baby, passes along the Appian Way with six thousand crucified men on crosses. That story was sold to Universal from a book written by a Commie and the screen script was written by a Commie, so don't go to see it.

Hopper was a virulent and extremely active red-baiter but she got her facts right here. The film was based on the novel by Howard Fast and the screenplay was written by Dalton Trumbo, both of whom not only were members of the Communist Party, but had been imprisoned for their unacceptable views in the early 1950s. To the upholders of right-wing values, the film not only looked dangerous, it must also have seemed an open act of defiance after years of intimidation.

Both writers were proven skilled, passionate, and committed story-tellers. They had both been deprived of their liberty in the recent past and were now creating a film about men fighting for freedom. The result was impressive. It was, however, surrounded by controversy from the very start.

Spartacus was the first film to have the name of a blacklisted writer in its credits and it has gone down in history as the film, along with *Exodus*, that marked the beginning of the end of the blacklist. Otto Preminger had already announced that Trumbo had written the script for *Exodus*, which was released later in the same year. But Douglas's step of including Trumbo's name in the credits was a huge one. *Spartacus* was the first film in thirteen years to carry Trumbo's name.

The very subject of the slave rebellion was inextricably linked with the idea of class struggle. The three novels written in English in the previous thirty years had been written by men who had all been actively committed to revolutionary politics. The making of this film must have looked like a show of strength for the Left which had been so undermined in the previous decade.

The Catholic enterprise, the Legion of Decency, was very strong. It had been created in the 1930s after the discussion of immoral films was raised at a Charities Convention in New York in 1933. Over ten million Catholics took the Legion's pledge against immoral films, and the pledge is worth reproducing as a representation of the attitudes of the time:

> I wish to join the Legion of Decency, which condemns vile and unwholesome moving pictures. I unite with all who protest against them as a grave menace to youth, to home life, to country, and to religion. Considering these evils, I hereby promise to remain way from all motion pictures except those which do not offend decency and Christian morality. I promise further to secure as many members as possible for the Legion of Decency. I make this protest in a spirit of self-respect and with the conviction that the American public does not demand filthy pictures, but clean entertainment and educational features.

This rejection of the filthy and immoral celluloid was very threatening for the film industry. On 7 June 1938 the House Committee on Un-American Activities was set up. (It is often referred to as the HUAC but more logically should be HCUA. The mistake is thought to have originated with John Howard Lawson, one of the Hollywood Ten who wrote about it.) On 27 October 1947 this committee started to investigate Communists in Hollywood. Ten 'unfriendly' witnesses, that is unfriendly to the committee, refused to answer questions, saying that this violated their constitutional guarantee of freedom of speech.

Fifty top film executives met in the Waldorf Astoria Hotel in New York the following month. They put out a statement that they had suspended the Ten (they were worried about their films being boycotted by the powerful Legion) and would not employ any Communists in the future. This statement initiated the blacklist. MGM suspended Trumbo and because he would not supply any names to Congress, he was jailed for a year in 1950.

With such a history, for embittered and embattled American left-wingers the resulting film must have been rather a disappointment. It was however immediately and immensely popular when it came out in 1960, and so it has remained. It was re-released on video, fully digitally restored, in the 1990s. The Catholic Church did not like it, but the film was probably helped by the fact that the President at the time, John F. Kennedy, went to see it in spite of the boycott, and declared he liked it. The support of the President of the USA was no mean endorsement, especially as the extent of his independence of Catholic teaching was not widely known at the time.

Visually *Spartacus* is extremely memorable: the final crucifixion scene is horribly dramatic; the sight of the Roman army advancing for the last battle (shot, incidentally, from half a mile away) is truly terrifying; the rows of regimented Roman soldiers stay in the mind's eye long after the film has ended. Charles Laughton and Peter Ustinov, so physically unprepossessing, sparkle across the screen. Some of the voiceovers are ponderous and clumsy but the dialogue is sharp, fast and often very funny.

It is not, however, by any stretch of the imagination a call to arms for the workers of the world. The critic Duncan Cooper summed up his own dismay with these words:

> The film makes rebellion an exercise in tragic futility rather than what it truly is – mankind's one genuine hope of achieving a human world society.

At the end of the film we see the thousands of slaves hanging on their crosses, suffering the most terrible death. Spartacus is among them, in a departure from the ancient sources where it is merely stated his body was never found. This image of suffering remains with the viewer, and the fact that Spartacus' wife Varinia and her child escape to freedom hardly makes up for the huge loss of life. Just as the Romans nailed up the slaves' bodies on crosses along the Appian Way, the film holds up the consequences of revolution for us to shudder at, and we do. What had gone wrong?

The scriptwriter

Trumbo, before the start of the blacklist, could command fees of $75,000 per script. Once the blacklist was announced an independent production company asked him to write a script for them for $3,750 which he accepted knowing he had no choice. And blacklisted writers (and soon there were many more than ten) meant that for small companies they could now afford the best quality writers for very little pay. Trumbo used friends as fronts at first, and after a while used different pseudonyms for each film. There was also a very complicated system of how work was paid for. There were no contracts to protect the writers. Trumbo could earn more as long as his identity was kept a secret, although the system kept the prices low. In normal circumstances a writer could command higher fees by advertising his own backlist. This was not possible for Trumbo since all his were under different names.

Once one of his fronts, Ian McLellan Hunter, received an Oscar for Best Original Screenplay for *Roman Holiday*, which Trumbo had written, but Hunter himself was later blacklisted. A script written for *The Brave Ones* under the pseudonym Robert Rich was awarded Best Original Story Oscar. Everyone knew Rich was Trumbo but he could not go and receive the award. Kirk Douglas knew of Trumbo and of his skills as a screenwriter and he also liked to keep his costs down. In 1959 five blacklisted writers were the sole suppliers of screenplays for the Bryna Company, Douglas's own production company, named after his mother.

Spartacus was a great disappointment to Trumbo – understandably so as there is little of the revolutionary leader in it, especially when compared to Fast's novel. Trumbo fought unsuccessfully to preserve his version of the film and was scathing about the final film's stress on the defeat rather than the achievements of the slaves. Instead of celebrating the astonishing success the slaves had had for so long over the phenomenal military machine that was the Roman army, against all the odds, the viewer sees only the final destruction of the slaves' hopes. What there is, which is very striking but ultimately depressing, is a lingering over the horrible crucifixion which resulted from the rebellion.

The blacklist itself contributed to the lack of a coherent view of the main character. Writers were not allowed on set and thus were not party to any changes that were made as the film was being made. Nor could there be discussions between the writer and director and producer as would normally happen. Sometimes there would be one initial meeting and then nothing until the shoot.

Changes to the screenplay are routinely made all the way through the shooting of films, so in this case these took place without the overview of the main writer. As he was not on set, Trumbo had little chance of seeing his vision realised. After seeing the first take of the film, Trumbo was appalled. He wrote an eighty-page report analysing what was wrong with it. Douglas described this as 'the most brilliant analysis of move-making I have ever read. It should be studied by every filmmaker.' And he goes on to describe events as if Trumbo's points were taken into account. They were not. Ustinov claimed that he rewrote many of the scenes for himself and Laughton, and that Kubrick simply shot them as suggested, which would confirm Trumbo's lack of influence. It is reported that Kubrick, having come upon a project already underway, kept himself to the physical aspects of the film and allowed the actors thrash out the dialogue by themselves, some of which is extremely funny. Olivier was apparently on set earliest, so it is due to his own energies that his character is so well developed in the film.

The answer to the puzzle of the lack of the revolutionary message in spite of the writers behind the project is that it was not their product alone. Kirk Douglas was the mover behind the project and the director was Stanley Kubrick – neither with a reputation for revolutionary politics.

The star

One can see the attraction of Spartacus for Kirk Douglas, quite apart from any political significance the slave-leader possessed. He was a glamorous hero. What more could any actor ask? More credit than has been attributed until now should probably go to Edward Lewis. He was a producer and friend of Douglas as well as a partner of the Bryna Company, and he suggested that Douglas read Fast's book. Douglas recognised the potential for a film immediately, and we saw his enthusiasm for the project in the previous chapter.

Douglas had just finished making *The Vikings*, and other recent epics had been very popular – *The Robe* (1953), *Samson and Delilah*, *Quo Vadis* (1951), *The Ten Commandments* (1956) – so he saw the opportunity for another success. Initially he went to United Artists, but they were already committed to another very similar project. They had opened negotiations to do a film based on Koestler's *The Gladiators* and were in fact intending to approach many of the same actors Douglas had in mind. The director was to be Martin Ritt, their Spartacus was to be played by Yul Brynner, and Antony Quinn was cast as Crassus.

Although at first the coincidence seems surprising, it should be remembered that Koestler's novel had been reprinted in the 1950s. The forthcoming movie was even announced in *Variety* magazine with a photo of Brynner posing as Spartacus and the declaration that the budget would be $5,500,000. Kirk immediately hurried his own production along. To make sure UA knew about it, he also sent a telegram to the head of UA saying he was spending $5,500,002 on his own *Spartacus*, just $2 more than the UA budget.

Douglas also hastened to get in touch with his actors and Laughton, Olivier and Ustinov all agreed to take part in Douglas's film. Douglas had persuaded his stars by sending each them a version of the script in which he/she appeared to have the largest and most interesting part. To make sure they beat UA they started to shoot as soon as possible. UA eventually abandoned their film and allowed Douglas to use the title *Spartacus*, which they had registered at the same time as *The Gladiators*.

Fast wanted to write the screenplay and sent in a version. The result was, according to Douglas, a disaster. Douglas and Lewis were both fans of Trumbo, who was a phenomenally prolific writer. One might say that he had to be prolific because, having been blacklisted, he could earn far less by writing. From the producers' point of view, of course, this made him even more attractive. Fast, on the other hand, seems to have disliked Trumbo intensely, and the fact that the latter was working on the screenplay had to be kept a secret from the novelist.

The original director of *Spartacus* was Antony Mann, but he was removed after a month's shooting. Douglas wanted the young Stanley Kubrick, who had recently directed him in *Paths of Glory*, and he got his way. Kubrick, like Trumbo, had huge criticisms of the final product, but Douglas is clearly happier with Kubrick's work as director. *Spartacus* of course is very closely associated with Douglas, so much so that the cover photo on his autobiography *The Ragman's Son* shows him as Spartacus, and it is the first film mentioned on the blurb on the back.

At the end of his autobiography, Kirk Douglas describes how forty years or so after the film a taxi driver still hailed him as Spartacus. Douglas's fame has diminished these days and he is probably more famous for being the father of Michael than for any of his screen appearances, at least with the younger generation. Indeed he ends the book with an incident illustrating this. A young woman runs up to him, and he internally congratulates himself on the great shape he is still in at seventy years old, but she exclaims, 'Wow, Michael Douglas's father.'

The film, despite Trumbo's and Kubrick's reservations, was not only popular but influential. The scene 'I am Spartacus' has been copied or alluded to in other films, such as *The Life of Brian* (1979), *Punchline* (1988), *That Thing You Do* (1996), *In And Out* (1997), *The Mask of Zorro* (1998) and most recently *Calendar Girls* (2003). It has been described by Trumbo's biographer Peter Hanson as 'The film's most iconic scene – and in fact, perhaps the most enduring scene of any Trumbo movie'. A Roman officer tells the captured slaves that they will all be crucified unless the body or living person of Spartacus is handed over. We see Douglas about to stand up, but at the same time Antoninus stands up and they both say 'I am Spartacus' at the same time. Then one by one all the slaves stand up and shout 'I am Spartacus'. Many, even if they have never seen the movie, know of this scene.

There is a story that one of Douglas's four sons, not Michael, was on tour in the UK as a stand-up comedian. He found it difficult to get the audience's attention. He became exasperated and called out indignantly, 'Will you stop talking? Don't you know who I am? I'm Kirk Douglas's son.' A man in the audience stood up and said, 'No, I'm Kirk Douglas's son,' and then another man stood up and said, 'No, I'm Kirk Douglas's son,' and then another man stood up …. The story is only understandable because the scene from the film is so famous.

The original scene makes the hairs on the back of your neck stand up even after you have seen the parodies of it. It was an addition by Trumbo, and one can read this refusal to betray the subversives and protection of the rebels from the authorities as a reference to the silence of the Hollywood Ten before the House Committee on Un-American Activities. It is powerful because we see a rebellion that is effective because of the numbers involved and invincible while those concerned remain united.

The director

At heart, the character of Spartacus is to me incompatible with Kubrick's films, for he is a man who undergoes a profound personal transformation, from good bright tough to heroic democrat-general. Such a character shift is unknown in all the director's films: The very most a person can change his point of view is to fall in love, and that is almost always fatal …. A second trouble with an all-Kubrick Spartacus is that the story violates his vision of human relations. Human relationships in Kubrick's films are rarely satisfactory and never warmly democratic. Spartacus and his fleeing comrades, living in a sort of ideal socialism, are an optimistic comment on human community, a topic Kubrick always approaches with distrust, pessimism, and futility (the natural confluence of reason and emotion.)

Norman Kagan, *The Cinema of Stanley Kubrick*[1]

At the age of thirty, when he started work on *Spartacus*, Kubrick had already made four feature films, *Fear and Desire, Killer's Kiss, The Killing* and *Paths of Glory*; but here he was taking over someone else's idea and was the second director chosen. But perhaps the biggest problem for the lack of artistic unity of vision was that Kubrick had read Koestler's novel, which was much closer to his own cynical view of humanity than Fast's more upbeat book.

It was Kubrick's biggest project to date: a $12 million budget, with superstars such as Kirk Douglas, Laurence Olivier, Jean Simmons, Charles Laughton and Peter Ustinov. The total cast numbered ten and a half thousand. The battle scenes were shot in Spain, the rest in California. And the total shooting time was a hundred and sixty-seven days. Spartacus, as depicted by Fast, is not Kubrick's kind of hero, at least as we see in his other films. And that tension between the different views of what Spartacus was like makes the film unsatisfying.

The initiative for the film came, as we have seen, from its star and executive producer, Kirk Douglas, who, as we saw earlier, as a Jew sympathised with the slaves. The lead character is presented more as a Moses-figure than a freedom-fighter. Trumbo thought it essential that the slave victories over the

Romans be presented on screen, but in fact all the audience ever sees is the final battle, their only defeat. Without seeing any of the previous victories, the reason for Crassus' fear of Spartacus is not clear, and there is no tension leading up to this great battle. The viewer has little reason to think that the slaves could win, having seen no sign of their invincibility in the past. As Duncan Cooper has described so vividly, there was also interference from Universal Studios, who provided the financial backing and distribution for Douglas's Byrna Company, because of their fear of the political climate of the day.[2]

As Kubrick himself said, there are thousands of decisions to be made when making a film, and if the director does not make them all and he is not on the same wavelength as the people making them, then it becomes a very painful experience. This was the case with *Spartacus*. Kubrick said, 'I am disappointed with the film. It had everything except a good story.'

But Kubrick was wrong. The one thing that ensured *Spartacus'* enduring popularity was its good story. The tale of slaves rebelling against all the odds against not just their masters, but the mightiest Empire in the world, with really not much on their side other than numbers, hope and rage, was the film's strongest point. The knowledge that some people do rise up and fight for their freedom is what viewers remember from the film, and what readers remember from Fast's novel and from Plutarch's *Life of Crassus*. That is the legacy of the story of Spartacus, not that he ultimately failed, but that he dared to fight.

Notes

Introduction

1. This is a quotation from one of his speeches, the full text of which can be found in *Gesammelte Reden und Schriften* vol. 9 (Berlin 1952), pp. 709-13. Liebknecht goes on to say 'Spartacus means every hardship and every desire for happiness, all commitment to struggle of the class conscious proletariat. Spartacus means socialism and world revolution.'

2. *Correspondence générale* 461-3. Letter 283, 5.4.1769.

3. Friedenstrasse 40-45.

4. 'Thus there was a natural tendency to identify, as gays, with a man who is credited with giving a sense of pride and humanity to a down-trodden group of human beings and taking arms against their oppressor and expoiters.' Frank Torey quoted in van Hoof (1993), p. 124.

1. The Outbreak of Revolt

1. *Ancient Slavery and the Ideal of Man*, translated by Thomas Wiedemann (Oxford 1974), p. 91.

2. *Slavery and Rebellion in the Roman World 140-70 BC* (London 1989), p. 101.

3. *Greek and Roman Slavery* (London 1981), p. 215.

4. 'Spartacus and the growth of historical and political legends', *Spartacus: symposium rebus Spartaci gestis dedicatum 2050 A* (Sofia 1981), pp. 64-70.

3. The First Victories

1. *Projecting the Past* (London 1997), p. 35.

4. Crassus

1. A.M. Ward, *Marcus Crassus and the Late Roman Republic* (London 1977).

2. Appian apparently confuses Marcus Lucullus with his brother Lucius who held the command against Mithridates; see B.A. Marshall, 'Crassus' ovation in 71 BC', *Historia* 21 (1972), p. 670.

6. The Creation of a Hero

1. Z. Yavetz, *Slaves and Slavery in Ancient* Rome (New Brunswick 1988), p. 126.

2. Shaw's translation (2001), pp. 14-15. Marx to Engels, London, 27 February 1861.

3. Donald Russell in *The Oxford Classical Dictionary*.

4. In his *Moral Essays* he contrasts the behaviour of Greek gladiators and barbarian ones. The Greek one of course behaves philosophically and sorts out his affairs instead of enjoying his last supper like the barbarians.

7. Spartacus in the Modern Imagination

1. As J.G. Griffith remarked, the major books on the period say little about Spartacus, 'Spartacus and the growth of historical and political legends', in *Spartacus: symposium rebus Spartaci gestis dedicatum 2050 A* (Sofia 1981), pp. 64-70. To take a more recent example, Michael Crawford's *The Roman Republic* for the Fontana

History of the Ancient World series (London, 2nd edition 1992), has Spartacus three times in the index but none of the references point the reader to anything longer than one sentence in his text about this revolt.

8. The 'Thinking Man's Epic'

1. 3rd edition 2000, first published Oxford 1972.
2. The full version of his articles on Spartacus published in Cineaste can be found on the website, The Kubrick Site: Duncan Cooper on 'Spartacus'.

Further Thoughts and Further Reading

Those who wish to learn more about the ancient Spartacus can do no better than to read the excellent *Spartacus and the Slave Wars: A Brief History with Documents* by Brent D. Shaw (Boston 2001). It contains a translation not only of many of the ancient sources about Spartacus, but also on other aspects of the life of slaves and gladiators and other rebellions. There is also a most informative and readable introduction, giving an overview of the ancient and modern Spartacus. (Another collection of sources in translation, this time with an invaluable discussion, 'Debates and Issues', was compiled by Zvi Yavetz, entitled *Slaves and Slavery in Ancient Rome* [New Brunswick, NJ 1988], but sadly this book is out of print.)

Brent Shaw has provided us with one of the most exciting accounts of the rebellion, since he gives us the words of the ancient sources in a clear and accurate translation and readers can see for themselves both the hostility and the admiration of the ancients for the rebels, as well as understanding that the voices of the slaves are silent. We comprehend their feelings only from reading about their actions: the numbers in which they flocked to Spartacus and his men, their resilience, ingenuity, bravery, and ultimately their suffering.

Having given us an overview of the impact of the story of

Spartacus on the modern world, in a narrative enviable for its combination of brevity and lucidity, Shaw remarks that the stream of inspiration dried up for some reason in the 1960s. More recent debts to Spartacus, seen only in comic books, some music and gay iconography,

> ... seem only to mirror marginal discursive reflections on an icon in decadence and decline. It seems that the romantic myth of Spartacus has had its day.

And a few pages later he continues in similar vein:

> Indeed, oppressed or downtrodden people have long dreamed of a better life and a more just social order, and these dreams have a history of their own. But the two-century history of freeborn peoples using Spartacus as a provocative symbolic means of thinking about their own dreams of liberation has come to an end, and that has much to do with the use, and abuse, of Spartacus as a symbol.

It is true that sometimes the uses to which the image of Spartacus has been put have diverged so far from the ancient figure that the result is almost unrecognisable, but Shaw has carefully and meticulously brought us back to the original sources. In so doing, he himself has helped to clear away the accretions so that a new generation can again see the pristine Spartacus and take heart.

In any case there is still interest in the story: a new TV mini-series based on Fast's novel, directed by Robert Dornhelm, was broadcast in 2004 by USA Network, starring Goran Visnjic (who plays Dr Luka Kovac in *ER*). Running for four hours, it was longer than Kubrick's film, although critics complained than too much of the four hours consisted of commercials. However this series continued the romantic myth of Spartacus, being based on Howard Fast's words, and starring the glamorous Visnjic who was chosen by *People* magazine as one of the fifty most beautiful people in the world.

For those who have not seen it, the film from 1984 of the Bolshoi dancing the ballet *Spartacus* with music by Aram Khachaturian is available on video. The music was composed in 1953, the year of Stalin's death. In 1948 Khachaturian, along with Shostakovich and Prokofiev, had been accused of bourgeois tendencies in his music. He pleaded guilty and was reinstated, but in 1953 he attacked this charge made by the Central Committee of the Communist Party, and it was withdrawn five years later. The music is instantly recognisable to many people because it was used as the theme tune of the popular UK TV series, *The Onedin Line*. It is gloriously exhilarating and this recording of the ballet is perhaps one of the most spectacular displays of passion, virtuosity and invention, as well as wit, that I have ever seen. For full effect it does however need to be seen on a big screen. The choreography is by Yuri Grigorovich, who was the artistic director of the Bolshoi Ballet for thirty years.

The choice of Spartacus for Khachaturian may have been an attempt to ward off criticism, since this was surely a revolutionary topic which would go down well with the authorities of the time. The depiction of Spartacus in Soviet scholarship would run to many volumes, but an excellent, short but rather frightening read is *Spartacus' Uprising and Soviet Historical Writing* by W.Z. Rubinsohn, translated by J.G. Griffith (1987), which is still available from Oxbow Books, Oxford.

There is of course much more to write about modern perceptions of Spartacus. Anton van Hooff has made an invaluable collection of material about the modern myth in his book *Spartacus* (Nijmegen 1993), which, unfortunately for most of us, is written in Dutch. However even non-Dutch readers will find his pictures interesting and his ten-page chronology (which he calls *Spartacia*) at the back of the book startling and useful. It starts in 1654 with Roger Boyle's *Parthenissa* and ends in 1992 with Jeff Wayne's CD *Spartacus*, passing through 1923 with *Spartakiada*, the Soviet Union's answer to the Olympic Games, and 1962 with *Son of Spartacus*, an MGM film directed by Sergio Corbucci, a sequel which has now disappeared. Perhaps most impressive, and most startling for me, since I grew up in this seaside town and know from personal experience that very few people outside Yorkshire have ever heard of the place, van Hooff includes a 1984 advertisement for a war-game on a shop door in Bridlington, East Yorkshire.

On Toussaint L'Ouverture, the successful slave-leader in the West Indies, C.L.R. James has provided not only an informative history, but, as is too often rare among academic books, a good read in his *The Black Jacobins* (new introduction by James Walvin, Harmondsworth 2001).

The role of Spartacus in Italian history is another major topic. Maria Wyke gives an excellent introduction to it, plus an overview of the making of the Douglas film, in ch. 3 of her *Projecting the Past: Ancient Rome, Cinema and History* (London 1997). A fuller and more literary analysis of the film can be found in Alison Futrell's article 'Seeing Red: Spartacus as Domestic Economist' in *Imperial Projections: Ancient Rome in Modern Popular Culture* edited by S.R. Joshel, M. Malamud, and D.T. McGuire Junior (Baltimore 2001).

Howard Fast says very little about the film in his autobiography *Being Red* (Boston 1990), which is hardly surprising since he was not very much involved in its making, but he is fascinating not only on how he came to write the novel, but on what life was like in this period of American history. Dalton Trumbo was once very famous, like Fast, but now is little known except to film buffs. His life, however, is very interesting and a recent book about him is *Dalton Trumbo, Hollywood Rebel* by Peter Hanson (Jefferson, NC 2001).

Compulsive and compulsory reading for anyone interested in the modern Spartacus are of course the three novels by Lewis Grassic Gibbon (*Spartacus*, reprinted by Redwords, London 1996), Arthur Koestler (*The Gladiators*, reprinted by Vintage, London 1999) and Howard Fast (*Spartacus*, reprinted by ibooks, New York 1996).

On the ancient Spartacus there is less to read at least in English, but apart from Brent Shaw's book, a good place to start is Keith Bradley's *Slavery and Rebellion in the Roman World 140 BC–70 BC* (London 1989).

Plutarch is in a way the hidden hero of this story. His *Life of Crassus* is essential reading for anyone interested in Spartacus and can be found in the Penguin translation of some of the Roman lives, *Fall of the Roman Republic*, translated by Rex Warner, introduction by Robin Seager (Harmondsworth 1972). Interestingly, until recently, like Spartacus, Plutarch has tended to be ignored in university courses since his biographies were viewed as little more than entertaining gossip, to be used only when more reliable sources were lacking.

Plutarch's lives *are* entertaining. He was concerned to show character and often did this by means of anecdotes, which most readers find fascinating and unforgettable. As he himself said, he was writing biography, not history, and what he left are masterpieces of observation and wit, as Shakespeare appreciated. If modern scholars have not displayed the perception of Shakespeare, this is hardly surprising. In any event, if you have never read any Plutarch you have a treat in store.

What is the relevance of Spartacus for the modern day? Perhaps it is simplest to answer this by quoting a scene from the film that was cut and then restored, where the Antoninus character played by Tony Curtis asks Spartacus:

Antoninus: Could we have won, Spartacus? Could we ever have won?

Spartacus: Just by fighting them we won something. When even one man says 'No, I won't' Rome begins to fear. And we were tens of thousands who said it.

To take just two examples, George Bush and Tony Blair have probably felt a little of that fear themselves.

Index

141